# FAITHCARE

# FAITHCARE

Ministering to All God's People
Through the Ages of Life

## Daniel O. Aleshire

The Westminster Press
Philadelphia

Scripture quotations are from the Revised Standard Version of the Bible, copyrighted 1946, 1952, © 1971, 1973 by the Division of Christian Education of the National Council of the Churches of Christ in the U.S.A., and are used by permission.

Book design by Gene Harris

First edition

Published by The Westminster Press®
Philadelphia, Pennsylvania

PRINTED IN THE UNITED STATES OF AMERICA

9  8  7  6  5  4

Library of Congress Cataloging-in-Publication Data

Aleshire, Daniel O., 1947–
    Faithcare : ministering to all God's people through the ages of life / Daniel O. Aleshire. — 1st ed.
        p.    cm.
    Bibliography: p.
    ISBN 0–664–24054–2 (pbk.)

    1. Pastoral theology.   2. Christian education.   I. Title.
II. Title: Faith care.
BV4011.A44 1988
253—dc19                                                87–30880
                                                            CIP

*For Jenny and Jonathan*
*With confidence that grace*
*will do its work with them,*
*and with hope that*
*the community of faith*
*will do its work, as well*

# CONTENTS

# FOREWORD

The wisest and best teachers and pastors seem always to be people who are able to look us in the eye, see into our hearts, and thereby receive us into their own lives. Somehow—it is not always clear exactly how—we feel ourselves to be known by them, not in a way that intrudes but in a way that accepts. They have an uncanny ability to hold us in their attention, see us as we are, and then invite us into relationship with them. The respect they give to us just by noticing us with care often sustains us and moves us, making it possible for us to learn and grow in ways we never thought possible. Beyond what they have to tell us—about the gospel, about the world, about ourselves—there is what they have to provide for us: a hospitable space in which to be the persons we are, each unique and individual.

Not every teacher and pastor we have ever had has been like this, even some of the very good ones. But if we have been lucky, one or two could be described this way, and some others come close. Teaching and pastoring are, after all, rather intimate forms of ministry. They inherently require quite personal involvements with people. Many factors are included in good teaching and pastoring, but at their heart lies the ability to be receptive to others, to understand, pay attention to, and discern with some clarity how life is experienced by those in one's educational and pastoral care.

How do teachers and pastors learn to do this? Some would say that it cannot be learned, that such sensitivity is an innate gift, a kind of natural *charism.* Perhaps there is something to this. Some people just seem to be born with this capacity, while others seem congenitally unequipped. But there is more to it than this. It is a capacity and a skill that we can nurture and develop. This happens in large part through being the recipient of such attention, understanding, and care ourselves. When we receive it, we can sense what it feels like and how important it is. Then we yearn to return it to others. Practice seems to be necessary if we are to enlarge these abilities. Finally, we can also be helped by learning certain ideas and theories about human beings, about how they grow and learn, about what influences and factors seem regularly to be important to take into consideration. At this point, certain books can be helpful, books like this one.

Educators and pastors have always known that understanding the people they teach and with whom they minister is important. That, perhaps, is the main reason why psychology books—books on human development, personality, and learning theory—have a prominent place on their bookshelves. Teachers and pastors have been aided in their understanding of people and in their ability to attend well to them by such books. But the help is not always as direct as one would hope. Most psychology books are not written *for* teachers and pastors. Their language is the language of theory, not practice. Their immediate concern is psychological description and theoretical coherence, not necessarily fostering receptivity to actual persons. Often they speak in such general terms about human beings that the uniqueness of the particular individual is swallowed up, while at the same time they focus on such limited dimensions of people's lives that the whole is lost to the parts. In addition, they are often written in such technical language that we find them difficult to comprehend, much less of use in discerning what is going on in the lives of the people we know and live with on a daily basis. Finally, something that is vital and central to people's lives, at least from the point of view of Christian pastors and teachers, is most often left out of consideration entirely: namely, the difference it makes that some people are people of faith whose lives are significantly affected by the fact that they are participants in the church.

As a result of all this, psychological theories often give us less help than we need. We need something else, something that helps us to benefit from psychological insights in the context of the situations in which we actually work, something that aids us by focusing our attention not on theory itself but on the people in our churches, in the light of the best insights that psychological understanding and faithful perception can offer. Such help is hard to come by. Most books that are written for church educators and pastors on these matters are largely watered-down rehashes of what the psychologists have said. They teach us theories we do not really understand and give us categories we end up either applying in simplistic and distorting ways or, more often, just ignoring.

Dan Aleshire's book is different. Written by a person who is both a teacher and a pastor and also knows psychological theory from the inside, *Faithcare* focuses precisely on the pastor's and teacher's fundamental task of paying caring attention to the children, young people, and adults who live with them in their communities of faith. The book teaches us what this task involves and, through countless vivid concrete illustrations, takes us into the mind and heart of one actually doing it. We not only get the idea of what it means to pay attention, we get the feel of it.

Simone Weil once said about attention that it "consists of suspending our thought, leaving it detached, empty, and ready to be penetrated by the object; it means holding in our minds, within reach of this thought, but on a lower level and not in contact with it, the diverse knowledge we have acquired which we are forced to make use of" (*Waiting for God,* p. 111; New York: Harper & Row, 1973). Paying attention to particular people involves exactly this. It does not mean applying psychological theories to particular people. Rather, it means opening space within ourselves to those people, allowing ourselves to be touched by them, making the effort to understand them. Psychological theory helps us to do this when it is kept "within reach" but is not allowed to suffocate attention. Paying attention to people in this way is extremely difficult to do. But it is vital to Christian love and care. We don't get a sense of what it involves from most psychology books. We do from Aleshire. We can learn from him how to do it.

Aleshire keeps psychological theory "within reach" for us.

He makes its best insights available to us. We can be introduced to it by him. We can understand a good deal of it through him. We can follow his lead to further study of it on our own. But most of all, we can be taught by him how to appropriate it for ourselves in a way that will actually help rather than hinder our primary educational and pastoral responsibilities.

This is a book I will put in the hands of all my students. It is one that will be read gratefully by pastors, professional religious educators, and church teachers throughout Christ's church. I will be turning to its pages over and again myself. Its marvelous readability makes *Faithcare* extremely accessible. Its integrity and depth makes every return to it very much worthwhile.

CRAIG DYKSTRA

*Princeton Theological Seminary*

# ACKNOWLEDGMENTS

While I was working on this book, people asked me what I was writing about. These questions proved embarrassing because I could never answer them in a word, or even a sentence. The writing reflected my convictions about ministry and people and had a definite purpose and perspective, but I was unable to find a word that adequately described them.

The manuscript finally was sent to the publisher, but the title page was still blank. I never found the word or sentence that described my commitments. What is a word or phrase for the process of attending to and ministering with individuals as they grow through the ages of life? What phrase aptly communicates the tasks involved in caring for individuals in their most normal days, when the crises that require the skills pastoral care provides are absent? What typical word refers to the ministry that people need as they learn from faith and life and attempt to construct new meanings and reinterpret old ones?

The creative people at The Westminster Press tried to find a word and ended up inventing one: faithcare. It is an invention that reflects a meaning in search of a word, not a word in search of a meaning. For me, "faithcare" is the task of attending to and caring for people who experience faith in the moments and movements of their lives.

The focus of this book is people—the people of God in particular. Faithcare is not a religious industry for the care of faith like health care is a scientific industry for the care of health. It is the sensitive process of attending to and ministering with individuals who are struggling—sometimes in the most ordinary of ways—to let faith emerge and grow in them.

Several people have encouraged and instructed me during the course of this project, and I would like to pay them some attention. Craig Dykstra initiated the process that resulted in this book. He has provided guidance and helpful criticism at each point along the way. James Dittes, Wayne Oates, David S. Schuller, and G. Temp Sparkman read drafts of the manuscript and gave significant amounts of constructive help. William Rogers, Kathryn Chapman, and E. Frank Tupper, colleagues of mine at Southern Seminary, have been effective conversation partners and good reactors to my writing, as have a special group of doctoral students at Southern Seminary.

This book tells part of the stories of many people. Their names are different, but their stories and lives have instructed me in the ways of both grace and faith. They have given their permission for the inclusion of parts of their stories in this book, for which they deserve thanks.

I would also like to thank faculty and administrative colleagues at The Southern Baptist Theological Seminary, who conscientiously work to maintain a seminary environment where ministry is a priority, truth is valued, integrity is standard, and Christian faith is expressed in both word and deed. The seminary has also provided excellent support, particularly through the competent work of Cindy Meredith and Jackie Morcom, who have typed and retyped the manuscript.

Finally, I would like to thank my family, who have shared this project. My wife, Jo, has had far more than her fair share of the householding and child-rearing responsibilities and has provided the critique the manuscript needed in the context of the support I needed. My children, Jenny and Jonathan, are frequently evident in this book. They are the most effective teachers I have ever had, and have evoked in me an appreciation for the work of God's grace, and the need to be introduced to that grace.

D. A.

*Louisville, Kentucky*

# PART ONE

## Paying Attention to the Way
## People of Faith Learn
## and Grow

Jonathan is three, and when he especially wants me to pay attention to him, he comes up to me, holds my face in his hands, and—eyeball to eyeball, nose to nose—tells me what is on his mind. It is hard *not* to pay attention to someone under these circumstances. Everything is clear. Jonathan wants me to attend to him and physically takes the matter of my attending into his own hands.

As Jonathan grows older, he will most likely learn the human capacity for indirection. He may want me to pay attention to him, but he will probably stop grabbing my face. His need for attention will be as intense, but it will be expressed more subtly. It is this way with the people at church.

Attending is an important dimension of ministry because people often express their needs indirectly and sometimes not at all. They do not always say, "Here is my need." They do not always even know their needs. Paying attention to people provides the information required for articulate expressions of ministry.

This book is about paying attention to individuals so the community of faith can help them learn a Christian way in the world[1] and grow toward maturity in faith. Its focus is on the kind of attending that informs ongoing programs of ministry, education, and missions.

Chapter 1 deals with the issue of *attending to people*. Ministers do not need to pay attention to every characteristic of the people with whom they minister, and some of the characteristics most easily noticed are more misleading than helpful. It is crucial, however, to attend to persons in ways that inform the ongoing programs of ministry, education, and Christian nurture. These expressions of ministry require attending to faith, development, and learning.

Ministers need especially to pay attention to *individual faith.* Other areas of life will be cared for elsewhere, but if the faith life of people is not dealt with at church, it will probably not be dealt with at all. Chapter 2 argues for the need to view faith not only as a theological reality but also as something that is experienced in human lives. How ministers pay attention to faith will influence how they go about many of the tasks of ministry.

Chapter 3 is concerned with *the nature of learning.* Over time, people learn things: about themselves, about their faith, about values and attitudes, about the world and its people, about action and work. They may not be learning what the minister hopes they will learn. They may not appear to be learning anything at all. But they are. Paying attention to the ways people learn can provide a better understanding of persons themselves, as well as guide the practice of ministry.

Ministers also need to attend to the ongoing process of *human development,* which is the subject of chapter 4. Most parts of modern society interact with individuals during only one part of life. Schoolteachers deal with children and adolescents more than with adults. Businesses deal primarily with adult employees. Physicians specialize so they work with children or adults, but seldom with both. It is different at church, however. Children, teenagers, young adults, middle adults, and older persons come together, often in the same room, Sunday after Sunday. The entire course of human development is on display at church, and this has both subtle and obvious influences on the way ministry is performed.

Paying attention to the way people of faith learn and grow is an important task of ministry. Attending appears disarmingly simple. It involves looking at people and seeing them for who they are and how life has touched them. "Look and See" was the first story in the first-grade reader. We have been busy attending all our lives. However, paying attention to people is still a surprisingly difficult task.

These next four chapters focus, both directly and indirectly, on the difficulties encountered when we pay serious attention to the people we teach and pastor. Attending to the faith experiences of individuals provides an essential insight and sensitivity for ministry. It requires us, however, to examine the lenses through which we view people, scrutinize our own perceptions of faith, and construct an appreciation for faith in its various expressions among the people of God. None of these tasks is easy. Each requires a discipline and exacts a toll. Attending to the learning experiences of people requires us to reevaluate our own understanding of how people learn what they learn, and what effects their learning has on their lives. We too easily assume that learning happens in classrooms, rather than family rooms and church hallways, and that the effects of learning show up in persons' thoughts more than in their relationships or prayers. Attending to the developmental experiences of people is difficult because it forces us to abandon assumptions about age groups in favor of perceptions about individuals. It requires us to give equal attention to all persons, regardless of age, and not to constrict our attention to certain people because they are a certain age.

Attending is certainly not impossible. Just as you read long ago, however, it requires us "to look" and "to see"—with an awareness of our focus, a sensitivity to our vision, and proper use of lenses that clarify our perception.

# 1

# Paying Attention
# to the People at Church

The people at our church were very much a part of a recent weekend, and the encounter of those two days put some things into proper focus and stretched others into a disconcerting blur.

It began Saturday morning with a funeral. A member of our congregation had died in his early eighties, leaving the legacy of a faithful and consistent life. He had joined our church in the 1930s and became a deacon in the 1940s. During child-rearing years, through productive middle adult years, and throughout retirement, he had been a dependable and thoughtful presence.

At the funeral, the members of his Sunday school class all sat at the front of the chapel as honorary pallbearers. This class of men, most of whom were now in their seventies, had gathered six times in the last three years for the funerals of lifelong friends and adult companions in faith. The wives of these class members were at the service too. They sat on the other side of the chapel, and their faces told the story of grief for a friend and sympathy for his spouse. Their faces also showed a silent worry, unexpressed and tucked away: Which member of the class would be next? The women brushed aside that worry, or at least tried to. It was time to tend to the needs of the new widow, to give her the gift of their attention and care.

After the service, the men of the class followed the casket out of the chapel and went outside ahead of it, to stand on either side of the walkway from the church to the hearse. The casket passed between them, and they stood a quiet vigil while people left the service. For these men, life had been more good than bad, more success than failure, more affluent than poor, more virtuous than sinful. These men did not have that sense of despair that comes to some people, who approach the end of life only to conclude it has been a tragic farce. I am not sure how faith grew in them over time, but somehow, it became a sturdy and enduring presence.

I left the funeral to return home and help with family preparations for our daughter's birthday party. She was turning nine and had invited several of her friends to our house for a celebration. The friends were from church and school, the two places in which Jenny is doing much of her growing up. It was an afternoon of laughter and giggles, lots of both, and a few tense moments. Some of the girls worried about being too readily excluded and needed assurance that they belonged within this circle of guests. Others felt awkward or reticent to join in and needed encouragement to participate. Everyone seemed to have a good time, but for some the good time came with greater difficulty than it did for others. At nine, a child is sensitive about fitting in, but the skills needed to negotiate the dynamics of a group are not yet mature. So parties flitter subtly between the giggle of delight and the laughter of tension.

On Sunday morning, our family gathered in the car. I asked Jonathan, then two and one half years old, where we were going. "Church!" he said in triple *forte.* "What do you learn at church?" I asked. In more subdued tones, he responded, "Jesus loves me this I know." It was one of those answers that mean nothing and everything. For Jonathan, "Jesus loves me" is nothing more than a song. The reality to which those words point is unknown to him. Perhaps, if Jonathan keeps learning the song, he will discover the Lover. But even if he discovers the Jesus who loves, how will he ever "know" the love of God and that God loves him? What kind of knowing is that?

After family members were in their respective Sunday morning places, I drove on to an area nursing home where I work with some volunteers who conduct a worship service. It is always an intense time for me. I never go to this task or experience these people without emotions. Nicholas Hobbs once wrote a book about the troubled and troubling child.[1] But for me, these adults are the troubled and troubling ones. They are old or infirm enough to require a nursing home environment, and most are affluent enough to be able to afford it. It is a good place—at least as good as these places can be—of thoughtful activities, common meals, and rooms decorated with possessions endowed with a lifetime of meaning. The past tense is the grammar of the present for many of the residents. Talk is of spouses who are no longer living and children who live in distant parts of the country.

These people value the opportunity for worship. When they recite the Lord's Prayer, they say it as if it has finally become their prayer. They are at a point in life when daily bread is an understandable request of God, and deliverance from evil is a sincere longing. The service is simple, and people from varied traditions find meaning in hyms poorly sung, liturgy barely seen, and a sermon hardly heard.

The residents of this facility are people who live beyond easy access to a church building. They are as marginalized as any group in American society. They pray more than other church members and live their days more reflectively. They have shed much of the materialism that many church people clutch tenaciously, but they are old and infirm; they can fill no volunteer roles; they cannot be present for Sunday worship. The churches that espouse a prayerful and reflective life seem to have forgotten some of their members who do these tasks best.

Following the service, I drove back to church for Sunday worship. Only this week, I had some responsibilities in the nursery. My job was to get the apple juice readied. Church, for these young children, was not yet a place where mystery and grace were topics of discussion. For now, there were friends to play with, experiences to encounter, and juice to drink. As I brought the pitcher to their room, it did strike me that community and participation and a common drink are not unlike the things they would consciously share as grown-up children of God.

After my nursery job was finished, I went on to worship. The sanctuary is an older place, full of dark woods and rich tones and seasoned with the stuff of weddings and funerals, choir festivals and youth celebrations, preaching and music, and bread and cup. I sat in the balcony.

So many people can be seen from there. I saw one couple who have struggled with their marriage and are trying to make it work. On one side of the balcony, a group of single adults were sitting together. Each of their marriages had come crashing to a halt in divorce. On the other side, the young people were sitting in the four pews they have claimed as their Sunday dwelling place. They are, for the most part, bright, engaging kids who are struggling with everything that is part of life in America. Down on the main floor, I could see this week's new widow, sharing worship with her children before they left for other cities. In the center section sat a handsome couple who are in the midst of successful careers; above them, in the balcony, sat a person who has experienced a series of career failures.

A good friend of mine was also sitting in view. His wife died four years ago, leaving him with the grief of her death and the task of raising a son and daughter. He is doing well now, but in parts of him as deep as the dwelling place of God's love, he always comes into this sacred room with the shrouded memory of his children's mother and the day her coffin rested in front of the chancel. That day he sat with a child on either side, incapable of holding all the grief he felt.

Where else but church can one encounter so many persons of such varied ages? School is not for most adults, and the workplace bars both the very young and the very old. But in the midst of the believing community, we can encounter everyone. Church is one of the few places in our society where the young and old, even the rich and the not so rich, gather together.

The people are so completely different. The gifts and burdens of life are so unevenly distributed. The gentle and the harsh are so randomly mixed among them. They are the people at church, and a part of ministry is to figure out how to pay attention to them.

## The Ministry of Attending

Paying attention is not so much complicated work as it is hard work. It requires a minister to spend more emotional energy noticing than getting noticed, and that is not always easily done.

There is a conflict in me when I have stood at the sanctuary door after leading worship, ready to greet the people as they leave. Do I use my emotional energy to listen for comments about how helpful the sermon was, or how meaningful a prayer was, or how good the service was? Or, do I use my emotional energy—even after worship leadership has drained much of it—to pay attention to people who seem to be troubled and anxious, or sullen and withdrawn, or joyful and animated? As the people leave, do I focus my attention on them and their needs, or do I look for the confirmation and affirmation that I need?

Paying attention to people requires some skill and sensitivity, but both of these are secondary to a commitment to give attention rather than attract it. Ministry, after all, does provide the platform to do either. Ministers have needs to be affirmed, but a commitment to the ministry of attending focuses energy on other people and their needs.

The ministry of attending yields two major benefits. One is that people who are taken seriously—people who are attended to—will feel blessed and affirmed. The power to bless, as Myron Madden has termed it, is one of the most potent resources ministers and priests have.[2] The second is that ministry efforts can be more precise, articulate, and effective when ministers pay careful attention to the people with whom they work.

A great deal has been written and said about how to pay attention to people in the process of pastoral care and in the context of group settings. Attending is crucial for good counseling and effective handling of group dynamics. Much of ministry efforts for hospitalized and bereaved persons depends on sensitive attending. Much less has been written, however, about the tasks of attending required for day-to-day, no-special-crisis, week-after-week ministry. Paying attention to people is as crucial for the ongoing education and program ministry of the congregation as it is for specialized counseling or short-term intervention ministries.

The ministry of nurture calls for attending to all the people, in the unfolding drama of the important but noneventful days

of their lives. Ministry requires paying attention to a kaleido-
scope of persons who are always changing. Life at church asks
caring ministers to detect the clues people give about themselves, but the clues are most often exhibited in the middle of
a crowd or behind closed doors. The ministry of attending is
important, even crucial, but it is also difficult.

## Paying Attention to People Is Difficult

Paying attention to people in their "normal" days seems
easy enough, doesn't it? "Helping" professionals are good at
doing it, aren't they? Doesn't this ability come easily to them?
While the first impulse might be to respond to these questions
affirmatively, a more reflective response leads to the conclusion
that paying attention to people is a very difficult task. At least
three reasons contribute to the difficulty: people are complex,
ministry is complex, and perception is complex.

### People Are Complex

Paying attention to people is difficult because humans are
complex, multifaceted beings. One may pay attention to what
people know, how they grow, what they own, where they are
from, what they do, how they look, what they like, how they
relate, what they believe, how they live, and what they worry
about. Each individual presents such a wide range of characteristics that it is difficult to pay attention to all of them.

Of course, a certain commonality exists in the human spirit.
Great art and literature communicate across time and cultures
primarily because of it. But this commonality is refracted into
complex hues and tones when it passes through the prism of
an individual life. What is true for the human family is not
necessarily true for one individual. The elegance of the simple
collapses into the muddle of the simplistic when individuals
attempt to understand others primarily in terms of common
characteristics.

Every person has a host of characteristics to which a thoughtful individual could attend. And almost every characteristic can
be present in an individual for a variety of reasons. Paying

attention requires not only noticing different characteristics but also identifying what those characteristics mean to the individual.

## Ministry Is Complex

The complexity of persons is only the beginning of the problem, however. Ministry is complex, too. Frequently, ministers and others who work in congregations must pay whatever attention they can while they are in the middle of many other demands. Consider one of those Sunday mornings when everything, it seems, needs some attention: A children's Sunday school teacher calls with a stalled car, an usher is trying to find a missing offering plate, and the minister needs to talk with the youth group about a problem in the upcoming retreat. In the midst of it all, someone brings a family who is visiting the church for the first time to meet the minister. All the other agenda items must be put aside, at least temporarily, so attention can be given to the people in this family. Now, put yourself in that minister's place.

You introduce yourself and ask their names. The woman takes the initiative to introduce herself, her husband, and the two children. They strike you as a handsome family. She also gives the children's ages. You acknowledge the children and comment on the eight-year-old daughter's dress. You ask, "Have you just moved to town?" They explain that they have, and you instinctively ask, "Where from?" The man responds this time; he merely identifies the city. You then ask, "Has work brought you here?" The woman nods affirmatively, and you look at both and ask, "What kind of work do you do?" The man identifies his employer, who has recently transferred him, and comments that his wife has left a difficult teaching job in an inner-city public high school and is taking a break from her career for their first year in their new community.

By now, you have used all your available time and must leave the conversation to get to other tasks. You have the discussion with the youth group, help the usher find the missing offering plate, check on the children's Sunday school class, and retreat to your office for a few moments before the worship service begins. For a moment, you think about that new family. What kind of information did you gather in the short time you had? Were the questions asked the ones that most contribute to understanding this family? Were they questions that paved the way to ministry, or were they casual questions that make for hallway conversations and little more?

Maybe you have never been in a situation like this one. I have, more than once. And more frequently than not, I have left the interaction thinking that, while I had elicited some information, I had failed to pay attention to the people themselves in a way that could have helped me understand them better. Failures like this are not caused by a lack of desire, or even a lack of skill. They are, more than anything, caused by the fundamental nature of ministry. Tasks, issues, and needs seldom arise one at a time, and seldom when there is ample time to think them through, consider the possibilities, and respond to them sensitively.

### Human Perception Is Complex

A third reason for the difficulty lies in the complexity of human perception. Perception begins by recognizing something, but it does not stop there. As soon as some new perception enters our consciousness, we begin a process of associating it with other information, categorizing it, and evaluating it. The human process of perception leads, almost inevitably, to interpretation. And the interpretation of information is a complicated phenomenon.

There are more scientific ways to discuss this issue, but none conveys its reality more than Jenny's account of the circus tickets. The circus had come to our city with its patented pomp and bravado, and our daughter, then five, wanted to go. The wish was granted, and tickets were purchased in advance. When Jenny saw them, she called me at the office and said, "Daddy, the tickets are beautiful. They are the prettiest ones I have ever seen!"

That evening, I looked at the tickets. I too was amazed at them, not because they were beautiful but because their appearance was so generic. They were computer-generated tickets with dot-matrix letters printed on some anonymous color of paper. Jenny had obviously seen the tickets through the trumpeted expectation of the circus, and they were beautiful. I saw them, as I had seen scores of similar tickets, no doubt biased a bit by their price, and they were plain.

Jenny saw the tickets as prettier than they were, and I saw them as uglier. Such is the character of human perception. It is not news that people looking at the same item see it differently. Sometimes this tendency enriches life, and other times it complicates it. Art and literature, for example, are enriched by the ability of people to see different textures of meaning in the same work. Juries, on the other hand, are frequently baffled by the tendency of different witnesses to describe the same event in widely divergent ways.

A circus ticket has a relatively concrete, objective character. It is not a terribly subtle or complicated piece of reality. Its shape, size, and color can be measured and documented. If something as simple as a ticket inspires conflicting reactions, what happens in the case of something very complex—like a human being?

Different people attend to different aspects of other people. Even when individuals see the same fundamentally important characteristics in other people, they may not interpret those characteristics in similar ways.

Paying attention to people is difficult, but it is not impossible. The problems associated with the complexity of people, ministry practice, and human perception are serious but not insurmountable. The problems and difficulties require some method for solving and simplifying, and most people have some way of doing just that.

## Dealing with the Complexity

Some individuals simplify the task of attending to people by paying attention to such obvious characteristics as gender, place of birth, occupation, and physical appearance. These qualities are easy to detect, every person has some version of

them, and sometimes they do provide accurate clues to understanding. I want to illustrate some of the characteristics people
frequently attend to, even if by default. Each illustration makes
the point that these characteristics may provide critical insight
about someone, but they do not automatically do so.


## *Gender*

Almost from birth, awareness of gender molds and influences the way a person is viewed by others. Even when young
children are not aware that they are male or female, people
begin making important distinctions about them on the basis
of gender. Female children are frequently treated quite differently from male children.[3]

Considerable debate exists about the degree to which gender influences human thought and behavior. Psychologists,
sociologists, and theologians all argue the point. The importance you place on gender for understanding other people will
vary according to the position you take in the debate. Do you
assume, for example, that gender is an important and non-
negotiable category for the understanding of individuals? If
you do, you may conclude that people cannot be understood
apart from the pain, strength, advantage, or disability they
perceive that gender brings to their lives. Or do you assume
that gender is not very helpful for understanding most people?
If you hold this assumption, you may not pay much attention
to persons on the basis of their gender and may think something is wrong with an individual who is deeply affected by his
maleness or her femaleness.

Either position can hinder an understanding of persons.
Gender is a gift of nature. People do not choose it, except in
the rarest of surgical instances. To make judgments about people on the basis of their gender may be more reflective of the
perceiver, and the perceiver's assumptions, than the person
perceived. Even as the most fundamental category of human
group membership, gender provides no fail-safe understanding of another person. It may be crucial for paying attention
to certain persons and highly misleading when attending to
others.

## Region of the Country

A perception that Americans seem to treasure is that people are different because they live in different regions of the country. The differences are perceived as so significant that conclusions are drawn about people based on the region of their origin or present residence. Southerners are slow; New Yorkers are rude; Midwesterners are—well, midwestern; Californians are laid back; Texans are, above all else, Texans. The United States is a country full of regional local color, with climates, ethnic heritage, and geography that differ dramatically. The differences, however, do not have as overwhelming an influence on fundamental human themes as many assume.

In several studies of beliefs and values that were carefully controlled for the effect of a region, region accounts for little or none of the variation in responses.[4] While political attitudes, tastes in food, cost of housing, and social customs do vary by region, the desires parents have for their children, the expectations parishioners have for their ministers, and judgments about what is morally right and wrong do not vary much from one part of the country to another. Yet many people persistently assume individuals can best be understood by their region, or the accent with which they speak, or the place they are most likely to speak of as home.

For some people, region is a basic part of their identity and they cannot be understood apart from their regional identification. There really are New Yorkers and Californians and, as the bumper stickers say, "native" Floridians. There are other people, however, who maintain a very limited identity to any region. They grew up in a military family, have lived everywhere, and claim nowhere as their home. Region may provide helpful information when trying to pay attention to some people, but only when they claim it as important.

## Occupation

Occupation is another piece of information that can lead either to understanding or to confusion. It is usually not many questions into a conversation following an introduction when individuals start asking, "What do you do for a living?" Occupation is, for many people, a fundamental part of their identity. To know that they are managers or machinists, contractors or chiropractors, teachers or lawyers is a key to understanding who they are. Erik Erikson suggests that vocation is one of two anchors (the other is relationships) to which adults can assign their identity.[5] The loss of job or retirement can become a major trauma for people whose identity is tied to occupation.

But for many other people, their work is little more than a means by which they make money. They have no investment in doing what they do and would quickly change if a better-paying job or better working conditions were offered them. Almost none of their personal identity is tied to the tasks they do to earn a living.

In a society of free choices, people assume that individuals have chosen their work and that it means something to them or they wouldn't be doing it. Such assumptions are frequently misleading. Occupation may signal more about the opportunities an individual has had than the choices that were made. Occupation may hint more at what an individual has been denied than what has been achieved.

*Physical Characteristics*

Several years ago, a family began visiting the church where I served as a part-time minister. The husband was injured in Vietnam and was physically confined to his motorized wheelchair. His wife confronted me a few weeks after they began attending when she realized I did not recognize her apart from her husband. She said, "My name is Carol, and I want you to know who I am when I'm not with Mike!" This was not the only time Carol helped keep me humble, but it was the first. And she was right. I noticed what was easy to notice. In the busyness of greeting the people who left the sanctuary at my assigned door, I noticed only the most obvious: the wheelchair-bound man and his family. I could not have paid attention to a more misleading characteristic. There is no way to ignore the requirements a quadraplegic family member places on life, but that disability, and those requirements, are not that family's most important characteristic. Church and school, schedules with two teenage children, and friendships and growth are the characteristics that most help a person understand Mike and Carol.

Obvious physical characteristics can so easily dominate one's perception of others that they distract attention from other characteristics that are far more crucial to an accurate understanding. I was calling the roll on the first day of class one semester, when I came to Sherrie and put an "ns" by her name to remind me as I was learning names that she was nonsighted. The next day, I scratched out the "ns," a good bit disappointed with myself. Of all the things that may be true of Sherrie, of all the things I could have paid attention to, why did I choose her inability to see? While I needed to be aware of this characteristic so I could teach a very visually oriented subject, statistics, it was not a characteristic in which she invested much of her identity or sense of self.

The obvious inadequacies of attending to these kinds of characteristics raise a question: Do ministers really use them more than they should be used, or have I just created a straw case to make my point? I think these characteristics really are overused.

Remember the conversation between the minister and the new family I posed a few pages back? How realistic did that conversation sound to you? Notice how many of the questions solicited information about occupation and region of the country, and how many of the comments reflected attention to physical appearance and gender issues. Of course, this conversation was an initial encounter, and it would be both inappropriate and insensitive to meet someone for the first time, say hello, and then ask about that individual's deepest fears or most faith-filled hopes.

My hunch is that in the busyness of ministry practice, especially in large parishes and congregations, attending to the people at church defaults to a survey of these kinds of characteristics. Sometimes, these characteristics work. The best way to know some people *is* by the region they claim, the occupation they hold, or their gender. But frequently, these characteristics misdirect attention. To attend to other people in such terms will leave them altogether unknown. Using them simplifies a difficult task, but it simplifies at considerable cost. These characteristics cover people; like a book, you can't always tell much about people by their cover.

If these characteristics are an unreliable guide for attending to people, what can provide more insight and help in structuring ministry efforts? I propose three areas. None of them can be assessed in an initial hallway conversation. But they are observable, over time, as people deal with life and share in the community of faith. They reflect the drama of life that occurs beneath readily observed characteristics. They are faith, development, and learning.

## Attending to Faith, Development, and Learning

These areas of life provide a valuable perspective for attending to people. This chapter began by telling you about some of the people I have encountered at church, and I would like to return to some of their stories in light of these three dimensions.

The man whose funeral I described was best known through his faith and faithfulness. Whether in attitude and spirit or in leadership and volunteer labor, this man could never have been known apart from his faith and the values faith brought to his way of being in the world. The death of my friend's wife radically intensified his struggle with the providence of God. Understanding my friend would have been impossible apart from the drama, fear, and passion of his faith.

Paying attention to people in terms of their faith seems obvious, doesn't it? It can be assumed, can't it? Not necessarily. Recently, I interviewed a panel of young people during a conference for youth ministers, and something that was said led to a conversation on sexuality and youth. Ministers began describing promiscuous sexual expressions in terms of cultural influences, low self-esteem, and other psychological variables. One of the panel members broke in on the conversation to say she thought that behavior was basically a moral issue, that young people do make decisions about sexual activity, and that church and faith can be important sources of influence in these decisions. The ministers in the room felt reminded, if not reprimanded, about the importance of attending to faith. Effective ministry requires a perspective on faith not only as a theological category but also as a fashioning force in human lives.

Some of the other people mentioned at the beginning of this chapter need attention in terms of their development. The little girls at the birthday party and the men and women at the funeral were all confronting developmental agenda. Nine-year-olds are dealing with peers and chums and how to be friends, and seventy-year-olds are dealing with the death of friends and how to deal with their own advancing years and a life with fewer companions. These are developmental events. They happen in the normal passage of years, and they raise concerns and fears that life in the community of faith can ease and calm.

To pay attention to development is to accept all the human family into one's perspective. Too many ministers are content seeing only the adults. A developmental perspective provides a sense of the drama of life and the richness of being human. Different movements of life bring different facets of the human spirit into focus. With each moment, each age, the gift of faith becomes more complex and clear. To pay attention to development is to attend to an individual in light of who the person has been and with a vision of who the person can become.

The children in the church nursery, Jonathan saying "Jesus loves me this I know" in his car seat, the older people at the nursing home, the adults facing failed marriages or careers— all have something in common: They are learning. A divorce requires learning new ways of adult life, new approaches to householding and parenting. Moving to a nursing home frequently requires learning how to deal with increased dependence on others and new patterns of life. Being two years old means that almost everything has yet to be learned and that learning is fun.

Paying attention to the ways people learn is crucial for ministry. Involvement in the community of faith over time should help people see the world and themselves differently, live out their affections for God, and align their lives with the purposes of God. All these hoped-for outcomes require forms of learning.

Paying attention to the ways people learn focuses a vision of ministry on characteristics that people need more than the ones they have. Learning pulls people into the future. To attend to the ways people learn is to see them in terms of the gospel's hope of what they should and can become. To attend to the ways people learn is to prod and support them, cajole and comfort them in the way of grace.

## Attending to Individuals

Human development and human learning are not easy dimensions to understand. Both are processes of change that take place over time, and both are highly individual. While there are patterns of learning, individuals apply them and prefer them in different ways. While there are common developmental themes, individuals create almost constant variations. Paying attention to people begins with a comfortable acceptance of their individuality.

The gift of individuality is among the most fascinating ways in which God has endowed the world, but for some reason people never seem very comfortable with it. In the beginning God made us unique, and we have spent an amazing amount of human energy attempting to identify the uniformity hiding beneath the uniqueness. Many seem to live with the assumption that individuality is really a surface issue. Down, at some deeper level, there are common themes that transcend individuality and expose it for the facade it is. Could it be that at the most fundamental levels of being human there exists nothing deeper, nothing more basic, than human uniqueness?

The following chapters will reflect both my psychological bias that human behavior does have fairly predictable patterns and my theological conviction that sin and grace as well as suffering and redemption exert profound influences on all people. But I hope they also reflect a guiding conviction that the foremost ingredient required in the ministry of attending is to see each human being as unique, one of a kind. Creation provides the root for such a conviction, and redemption provides an environment in which it grows comfortably.

Paying attention to people is not the lost skill of ministry, whose rediscovery promises a new day with a new way. Paying attention to people is not something new to ministers who care about the people with whom they work. It is, however, a crucial ingredient in the ways people encounter others and construct ministry in ways that take others seriously and faithfully.

I invite you to pay attention to the people who question and celebrate, grieve and believe, and to envision expressions of ministry that will help them learn the lessons of faith and grow to maturity as faithful people.

# 2

# Paying Attention
# to the Way of Faith

Sarah and Will have been friends for seven years now. They are both nine years old, and the environment in which their friendship has been nurtured is church. Both of them attend just about everything: Sunday school and worship, Sunday night educational activities, Wednesday night choir and missions education, special Saturday events, and camp in the summer. Talk of faith is all around them. They are both "believers"—they can tell you about Jesus and John, Moses and Jonah, God's love and God's world. They are bright children who have faith forming in them and who will quickly learn its lessons.

Samuel does not learn well. In fact, that is one of the most obvious features about him. He is a retarded young adult who lived with one of the families in our congregation for several years. Because he has a very limited vocabulary and is reticent with strangers, he depended on the people at church to initiate interactions. Some church members provided a Sunday school class for him, and during worship he would sit in the balcony with the father of the family with whom he lived. He usually spent his time during the service turning through the pages of the hymnal, one at a time. In spite of his limitations, Samuel seemed to enjoy church. What, I have wondered to myself, can faith mean to Samuel? What human capacities does faith require?

Ann is a young adult who lives with problems different from Samuel's. She is bright, very bright. But life during her entire adulthood has been more struggle than celebration. She has been hospitalized for depression more than once and has suffered the consequences of her disease. Ann is a fighter. Her ongoing traumas have left scars, but she has not let them capture her will to overcome the pain or redefine life. She has occasionally been on friendly terms with the God of grace, but she has been in more than one wrestling match with that God as well. The raging in her seems to be a battle between her longing to love God and her anger at a God who has not moved more aggressively to ease her pain. She also feels a tension between her need for people of faith and her frustration that those people cannot—or, more fearfully, will not—give her the help she needs.

Robert is middle-aged and has built a successful business. He is a leader in the church who takes faith experience seriously and is sensitive to the ways in which being Christian and being in business mix and conflict. He reflects on his financial success and the poverty of others. During the last five years or so, his faith seems to have deepened or widened; it has become more intimately a part of him. He is more confessional about his commitments and more committed to the practice of his faith.

Betty is about the same age as Robert, but her life has been changing in a painful direction over the past two years. Her husband is an Alzheimer's patient, and the deterioration in his ability to deal with the world is growing increasingly obvious. The adult businessman she married is becoming a big preschooler. There is no remission in the advance of his disease and little relief from the demands for her care-giving. Faith, for Betty, includes a struggle between acceptance of what is and a piercing question about why life has turned in this direction. She teeters between gratitude for the people in her faith community and frustration that they do not know how to respond to her private horror. Her faith is being hammered and bent into shapes she has never known before.

These six people raise a number of questions about faith. What is it? Why do people have faith? Is faith the same experience for everyone? How does faith grow? How can faith be influenced? The responses to these questions will influence one's perceptions and practice in ministry. This chapter will raise more questions than can be answered, but paying attention to people of faith keeps bringing questions to mind—and to heart.

## Images and Definitions of Faith

Faith is mystery. One day, the cloud of unknowing may be dispelled, but not yet. We know the aroma of faith and its feel, we know its movement and its grasp of us. We may grow accustomed to its presence in our lives, but faith remains a mystery. And, like Ezekiel's wheel within a wheel, it is a mystery within a mystery.

In the churches in which I grew up, we sang a gospel hymn called "Faith Is the Victory." From the battleground of life, we were reminded that faith brought hope, faith brought order, faith brought resources, faith brought help, faith brought victory. In more than one way, it does. Growing up with that song, however, misled me into thinking that faith was more identifiable, more easily understood than it is. Faith is more mystery than victory. No other reality is more familiar or mysterious to me. I live my life in the middle of faith, and on its edges, but find it impossible to trace its path through any one person's life or to propose the conditions that will certify its growth for another.

As I write about faith, several emotions quickly surface. Perhaps the syntax of these feelings can be more instructive than the grammar of logic. To write about faith evokes a respect in me. It is similar to the feeling I get when I examine some sturdy relic of the past. I hold it with care, and I sense in its touch the years, the others who have held it, the meaning, the drama of people and time and history. To write about faith troubles me. I do not want to cop out intellectually by saying it is mystery, but I know it—at least some form of it—too well to say anything else. It is a reality that is at once a pervasive human phenomenon and an intensely personal experience. Talk of faith as an abstract human experience is too esoteric, and talk of faith as a personal reality in me is too exhibitionistic. To write about faith has more the feel of poetry than prose. Rhythm and form are as fundamental to its expression as analysis and deduction. To write about faith is a confessional act that grows from my own longings. I want the people at church to discover the way of faith in the world, to be strengthened and nurtured in that way, to live responsibly by the disciplines of that way, and to experience the wholeness of that way. To write about faith is to invite readers into a holy space, where mystery is permitted and a sacred tentativeness comes naturally.

Ineffable reality, tender mystery, durable imagination, gift of grace, sturdy embrace, surprising transformation, grasper of the Not-Yet: faith is, in one way or the other, all of these to me. But poetry and longings must be articulated into the prose of ministry efforts. However much faith is ultimately a mystery, it is important to explore those parameters and contours in it which can be charted.

People have tended to examine faith in one of two ways. Some have argued that faith is best understood in terms of the paint, brushes, and technique people use to create a picture of life's meanings and movings; others explore faith by examining the painted picture. The kind of faith I most want to address is more fixed in the painting than in tools and techniques. I live my life before a mural that is the Christian tradition and want to speak of faith as I have seen it. The mural is not finished, and I will use a brush to add my portion to it, as do all other Christian believers. I must learn the techniques, but I must paint my part with an awareness of the work others have done over thousands of years.[1]

## Questions About Faith

I want to introduce some issues about faith by raising several questions and reflecting a few of the responses to these questions that exist in an extensive literature about faith.[2] The ways of answering these questions are not necessarily competitive with each other. They represent shades of emphasis. Many people would affirm all the responses listed under a single question, while others would take sides and declare a defined preference. These questions help set the agenda for a perspective on faith that informs the way people learn and grow at church.

## *Where Is Faith?*

One way of responding to the question "Where is faith?" is to say that faith is "out there"—in the church, in the community of faith.[3] Faith is something that exists among the people who are called to live according to God's will and purposes. One enters faith by participating in the community of believers, by accepting their prescriptions of truth, by acting in ways that conform to and support the purposes of this community. In this sense, faith is an external, objective reality in which the individual participates. When viewed this way, the primary idiom of faith includes its content or doctrine and the actions to which that doctrine directs its subscribers.

A second possibility is that faith is "in here"—something within the person. It is a way in which the individual views the world, identifies fundamental powers, determines values of life-shaping importance, and organizes the character of life and one's place in it. When faith is viewed this way, its primary idiom includes the grammar of experience.[4]

Still another option is to emphasize that faith is from beyond, or "up there," as the ancients would say. Faith, like grace, is something authored by God and bestowed by God in the lives of persons. Faith is thus something to be received from God. It is not a religious work the believing person does, or a way of looking at the world fashioned primarily by community or individual. It is a gift from the God who transcends boundaries and who gives persons eyes to see and ears to hear this work. When viewed this way, the language of faith requires the grammar of stewardship. Faith is a sacred trust, and a part of the individual's response to it involves its care and upkeep.

The emphasis that persons place on these different answers will influence how they view the learning and growing dimensions of individual lives at church. To emphasize the "out there" perspective would call for approaches to learning that best facilitate the individual's acquisition of the doctrine and behavior espoused by the community of believers. An emphasis on the "in here" possibility could lead to nurturing persons in ways so they better experience faith and learn its source of power in their lives. If the "up there" option is valued most highly, people might facilitate mystical experiences to help individuals sense the presence of the transcending God and teach them the disciplines by which individuals care for the faith that has been entrusted to them.

### What Is Faith?

Some contend that faith consists primarily of a set of ideas to which the individual is committed as true. Faith is holding firm to a body of doctrine. It is, more than anything else, a matter of the head. Others describe faith more as a matter of the heart. It is the way by which people feel their way toward God, experiencing God's love and responding with their own. Still others would argue that faith is most fundamentally a way in which persons order their behavior in the world. Faith, at its most basic level, deals more with what people do than what they think or feel. Orthodoxy is better seen in behavior than ideas. When feelings and ideas drift away from God, behavior can keep faith faithful. Many, perhaps most, would define faith as a combination of some or all of these dimensions.

The responses persons bring to the "what" question will also influence ministry to the persons growing in faith. If faith is primarily holding to doctrine, nurture will focus on clarifying content and developing allegiance toward propositional truth. Those who cannot think well will not be as able to mature in faith as others who can think well. If faith is primarily a matter of the heart, nurturing faith requires helping people to identify their own emotions and to become aware of the feelings of others. People who have emotional problems are the ones who may be stunted in faith. If faith is fundamentally behavioral, anyone who can be coaxed, coerced, or cornered into right behavior can be numbered among the faithful.

### Why Do People Have Faith?

One way of viewing the purpose of faith is that it provides order and structure for life. Faith is, thus, a meaning-making activity and becomes the individual's way of responding to the deep and subtle "why" questions of human existence. Faith is a religious enterprise because it is the tool people use in responding to questions that are fundamentally religious.[5] Another way of describing the purpose of faith is to conceive of it as the means by which people become related to God. Faith involves a person's ability to perceive God's initiative in his or her life and the intentional response the individual makes to that initiative. In this emphasis, meaning emerges from this relational, intentional way of responding to the presence of God.[6] Still another idea about faith's purpose is that people have a "God-shaped" vacuum in their lives that creates a fundamental longing only God can meet. Faith is the means by which people fill this vacuum, the process by which wanderers in the wilderness find the manna they need for life and are able to partake of it.

The processes of meaning-making, of intentional relationship, and of meeting fundamental needs overlap at certain points and are distinctly different at other points. Meaning and relationship, for example, may be the aspects of faith that fill the vacuum. Or relationship with a God who is ultimately trusted may reduce one's need for meaning-making. A steady trust in God may generate confidence, even in the midst of meaninglessness.

### Who Has Faith?

Some people think that everyone has faith. While the content, expression, and use may vary, everyone has faith. The object of faith may differ, from God to politics to the economy to values to almost anything, but everyone has some form of faith.[7] Others contend that only certain people have faith. People who have faith hold to particular affirmations and are grasped by certain realities. Faith is not a human universal; it is a peculiar and particular way in which some people find their way of being in the world.[8]

If a minister divides the world into those people who do not have faith and those who do, some ministry effort may be devoted to the process of inviting people without faith to claim it. Ministry is calling people to conversion. If faith is held by all—although focused on different objects—ministry may involve helping persons shift their faith focus from some less noble object to a more true and enduring one, as defined by a doctrinal affirmation about the value of objects. Nurture becomes a focus of ministry in this perspective. Conversion and nurture can be friendly co-laborers, but Christian traditions have tended to embrace one while holding the other in some suspicion. Perhaps part of the tension reflects differing assumptions about who has faith.

### How Does Faith Develop Over Time?

One view is that faith develops in a quantitative way. Thus, a mature faith is bigger—represents more faith—than a less mature expression of faith. Jesus' teaching about the faith the size of a mustard seed sets the stage for this analogy. Mature faith means more faith, and the amount of faith changes over time.[9] A second contention is that faith does not develop in the sense that human bodies or thought develop over time. Faith is a gift of God. It is shaped by life and tradition. Faith is "remembering God," and it changes as attention and memory change. It does not change in the predictable ways developmental processes bring about change.[10] A third perspective is that faith develops in more qualitative than quantitative ways. The growth of faith is more like a caterpillar's growth into a butterfly than a colt's growth into a horse. Shifts in form, appearance, and function vary dramatically from one stage to the next. The differences are so great, in fact, that it may be difficult to recognize the faith in one stage from the faith of the preceding stage.[11]

Each of these three perspectives about the way in which faith changes over time will influence ministry strategies. If, for example, faith grows quantitatively, then people can be taught and motivated to make faith grow. Like athletes, they can be trained, disciplined, and coached into growth. If, however, faith as an act of God's grace involves remembering, then ministry needs to help people live reflectively and openly to the presence of God. Finally, if faith grows by moving through a sequence of qualitative stages, then ministry entails sensitivity to the complexion of faith at various stages, patience with people who cannot be rushed through one phase to the next, and encouragement of people who experience the crisis of losing one kind of faith before the next kind emerges.

## A Composite Perspective

These questions, and the possible answers they attract, identify some of the issues that definitions of faith must address. A perspective selects from possible options in order to provide a focus and to identify the boundaries for a concept. I want to present portions of several definitions of faith and argue for their validity as a composite perspective. These definitions provide different angles of vision on the phenomenon of faith and, as a group, provide an informed perspective more than do competing claims.

*Faith is an openness to God.* In some way or another, faith evokes a person's openness to God. While it may be the work of faith to create this openness, I lean more toward the idea that faith provides individuals with the ability to perceive or experience the openness God has created. C. H. Dodd, in his commentary on Romans, characterized the meaning of faith for the apostle Paul as "an attitude in which . . . we rely utterly on the sufficiency of God. It is to cease from all assertion of the self . . . and to make room for the divine initiative."[12] Dwayne Huebner, in a similar vein, characterizes faith as an "awareness of God's presence. . . . Faith is remembering God."[13]

*Faith is relational, transforming participation.* Faith also involves the relationship of an individual both to others in the community of faith and to God. Faith is openness, but it is not passive. It calls for an intentional participation of faithful people with other believers and active identification with the purposes of God. Faith can thus be construed, in C. Ellis Nelson's words, as a relationship with God that derives "its meaning from the object of that relationship—God,"[14] involving an open-ended process of critical review and reconceptualization of doctrinal affirmations, and ongoing participation with the community of faith. Sara Little contends that "within . . . relationship, the person is formed and re-formed into the likeness of the object of faith. . . . In that revelation and response, where faith is established as the relationship between God and his people, we have the uniqueness of what is known as Christian faith."[15] Craig Dykstra has emphasized that faith is "appropriate and intentional participation in the redemptive activity of God."[16]

*Faith involves meaning-making.* Faith also has some dimension to it that relates to the human phenomenon of meaning-making. Most people have some desire to make sense out of life or to discover the meaning that exists in life and the world. James Fowler contends that faith is a way of knowing and construing that underlies a person's frame of meaning, that is generated from the individual's attachments or commitments, and that thereby endows relationships and the patterns of everyday life with meaning.[17] Faith has to do with the human process of meaning-making, and according to Sharon Parks this meaning-making "frames, colors, and relativizes the activity of the everyday."[18]

*Faith changes.* Faith—as openness, as relationship with God and others, as intentional and appropriate participation, as a meaning-making activity—is not static. The way an individual experiences and expresses faith will change during the course of adolescence and through adulthood. Fowler, for example, has described faith as "evolved and evolving."[19] Faith has a quality of movement to it. It involves the transforming work of God, which changes people and makes them capable of new and different forms of intentional response. Life situations change and bring different pains and burdens, which challenge old meanings and evoke new meaning-making activities.

## Ministry with People of Faith

Each of the questions about faith, and the composite perspective I have offered, paves the way for a discussion of ministry with people of faith. I want to suggest a characterization of faith that informs the ministry approaches proposed throughout this book.

Faith is a multifaceted phenomenon. Faith is not just *any* thing, but faith is more than *one* thing. This chapter began with references to six people who vary in their ability to learn, in their developmental point in life, and in their struggle with the issues of Christianity. Each is capable of a form of faith, even though the forms and expressions may be very different. Faith, at least in my understanding of the Christian tradition, is a response to an initiating, pursuing God. The God who longs after the people of creation will accept, as faith, whatever response these people are capable of making to that initiative.

### Components of Faith

People respond to God's initiative differently, but their response will be drawn from some basic human abilities. One of these is the *ability to think.* For people whose ability to think is unimpaired, the ideas they affirm will influence the ways in which they see the world, make judgments about the right, discern the issues of life, and constitute meaning. Ideas can even influence behavior—if in no other way than to trouble an individual when he or she acts in ways that are contrary to espoused ideas or beliefs. Ideas do not always determine behavior or feelings, nor are they the key to the expression of faith, but they are part of it.

Another ability is the *capacity to feel.* Faith includes the capacity to trust, to live in a posture of loyalty to God. Trust has an undergirding affective dimension to it. Christian faith also has something to do with the love of God, neighbor, and self. These ways of responding are all more affective than cognitive. The work of God's spirit in human lives has, according to scripture, a strong sense of the affective—joy, love, peace, patience, gentleness, kindness (Gal. 5:22–23).

A third dimension to this response to God is the *ability to behave.* Faith and works, according to the epistle of James (2: 14–26), are inseparable. The first words of Jesus' invitation to people to become disciples called them to a behavior: leave, follow (Matt. 4: 19–20). And the last words of the resurrected Christ commissioned the disciples to another behavior: go, make (Matt. 28: 19).

While there is value in attempting to identify the process of "faithing" in terms of component parts, it can be terribly misleading. It is the equivalent of describing a pound cake by its ingredients. To know that a cake is made from eggs, butter, milk, sugar, and flour may be interesting, but it is very difficult to construct a sense of the texture or taste of a cake from this information. Faith is comprised of thinking, feeling, and behavioral elements, but they interact with one another and impact one another in ways that make the experience of faith something different and unique from its ingredients. Thinking and feeling merge, in the processes of faith, into what some call convictional knowing[20] or imaginative knowing.[21] Feeling and doing are molded into active expressions of commitment and spiritual disciplines that would be entirely misunderstood if perceived as behavior alone. Education for faith needs some sense of component parts because people best learn how to think, feel, and act in different ways. But the goal of education for faith is mature *faith*—not mature thinking, mature feeling, or mature doing.

To the extent that a person can think, feel, and act, faith includes all these dimensions. Most people on earth and in church are capable of all three dimensions of responding to God. For these people, faith does entail a way of perceiving the world, a process of meaning-making, a participation with others who share the belief, an intentional participation with the perceived purposes of God, the ability to create room for the divine initiative and remembering God.

To the extent that disease, genetics, or the trauma of life has deprived a person of any of these abilities, whatever resources remain can become the stuff out of which the creative grace of God can craft faith. The God of the Bible keeps calling on those who have eyes to see and ears to hear to look and to listen. But to the blind and the deaf, the same God gives a way of seeing and a way of hearing.

This characterization of faith, I realize, is also a characterization of grace. These two crucial elements are rightly separated in theological study, but they become intertwined in human experience. Faith is not just an individual's response to grace, it is an act of God's grace itself. We are saved "by grace through faith." Both grace and faith have their source with God and find their destination in people's lives.

## Faith and Ministry

The way in which faith is understood has a profound effect on ministry practice. Much of a minister's attention to the people at church takes focus in their faithfulness—their faithful response to God, their practice of faith in church and society, and their experience of faith as individuals sorting through the joy and pain of life. The way in which a minister defines faith will cast a long shadow over the concepts of learning and development that are deemed relevant to the tasks of ministry with persons. A concept of faith will also influence some of the goals a congregation may set for its ministry and the strategies it employs to implement those goals.

Faith is tender mystery, ineffable reality, gift of grace, sturdy embrace, and much more.

One image of faith I have is that faith is, first and foremost, a work of God. God has been and continues to be creative, and that creative genius shows up in the way God works faith into individual lives. Creation has pattern and order, but it also has an infinite capacity for variety. A second image of faith is that it takes root in human lives and emerges in the context of human abilities and limitations. Faith is incarnational; it is not a spiritual gift from God that is housed in persons but not influenced by human nature. To the extent that people are individuals, the aspects of faith they emphasize and the covenants of faith that most readily influence them will be individual.

So ministry that encourages people to grow in faith must be able to recognize faith in authentic individualized expressions. Ministry that nurtures faith must be open to the God who makes people unique. It must also be sensitive to people who have experienced God's grace in a variety of ways and who struggle with a response that is congruent with their own personhood. Ministry must also seek to be a continuing invitation to people to allow their faith to mature as they themselves change in response to life's demands and reprimands.

Faith is durable imagination, surprising transformation, grasper of the Not-Yet, and much more.

Ministry with people of faith is teacher and midwife, counselor and comforter, interpreter and encourager. Paying attention to people of faith requires standing at the intersection of the uniqueness of every human being and the intensity of God's passion to redeem each of them. It is there, in this intersection, that faith is fashioned.

# 3

# Learning in the Community of Faith

*Then you will understand righteousness and justice*
  *and equity, every good path;*
*for wisdom will come into your heart,*
  *and knowledge will be pleasant to your soul.*
                                        —**Proverbs 2:9–10**

The biblical image of "knowing" has little similarity to modern perceptions of knowing as the possession of information—like some commodity to be banked and bartered. The Bible's use of knowing conveys a more experiential basis. What moderns may divide into knowing, loving, and experiencing is blended together in ancient Hebrew thought. To be people of faith is not just to know about God; it is to know God. To know God is to experience the Presence, to express love, and to hold tenderly the mystery of that encounter.

Faith requires a relational knowing because Christian truth is not some substance to be owned. Rather, it is something with which Christians live in relationship, something to which believers are betrothed. Parker Palmer writes that, in our spiritual tradition, "the origin of knowledge *is* love."[1] The kind of knowing that love breeds is different from the kind of knowing that power or pride breeds. It is a knowing in which truth is engaged and not possessed. To live in relationship with truth means that truth is given a chance to know us, and when the truth knows us it will change us. We become vulnerable to its power in our lives.

This image of knowing is not far from the one drawn in the wisdom literature: "for wisdom will come into your heart, and knowledge will be pleasant to your soul" (Prov. 2:10). The kind of knowing that faith requires does not stay in our heads. It invades our hearts and actions as well. The knowing that faith evokes is pervasive.

How do people come to this kind of knowing? I would propose two ways: The first is a gift of grace, and the second is a product of learning. When the gift is received and learning is attempted, faith-knowing can emerge and mature. This chapter is about learning.

Learning in the context of Christian life involves the process by which people are introduced to the Christian community—its stories, people, ways, and vision of the world—and incorporated into that community, experiencing its fellowship, participating in its mission, and moved by its passion. It is through learning that individuals acquire the skills, sensitivities, information, and attitudes that enable them to identify with and function within the believing community. To learn is to mature in the capacity to live in relationship to the truth, and to respond with obedience to that truth. Learning occurs within the interaction of the Christian story, community practice, and the individual's changing awareness of self and others.[2]

Learning in faith is a comprehensive enterprise. It is not limited to those events when a time is set and a teacher is designated. It embraces a wide range of human experience and perception. Learning in faith is a community enterprise. It is something people do in the presence of others, in response to shared prompting, common longings, and diverse reactions. Learning in faith is not a special spiritual enterprise. It takes the ways in which people learn anything and transforms them into ways by which people stay their hearts, minds, and actions on God.

Most importantly, learning in faith is learning in *faith.* The hoped-for result of learning in the Christian tradition is faith-knowing, not a pile of religious information. Learning in faith cannot be addressed apart from a perspective on faith. Chapter 2 proposed a perspective, and in it I argued that faith has affective, behavioral, and cognitive dimensions. Each of these dimensions can be influenced by learning, but each requires different approaches to learning. People learn affective lessons, for example, differently from the way they assimilate factual information.

This chapter addresses the issue of learning in faith in terms of the processes of affective learning, behavioral learning, and cognitive learning. Each process contributes to a kind of knowing that is rightly called faith-knowing.

## Affective Learning

Learning the way of faith begins, I think, with the affective dimension: tutoring the ability to love God and others, nurturing the capacity for trust and hope, and encouraging the growth of convictions.

Emotionality is an intrinsic part of the process of believing. James Dittes argues that beliefs themselves do not have a power that fashions human longing and response in the world. Rather, beliefs are derivative. They are outward reflections of inward "processes, postures, and passions."[3] It is this inward posture and passion that gives believing the power to form us and perhaps, when mixed with grace, the power to transform us as well. Passions motivate and influence, and we would do well to be informed about them and to tutor them, if that is possible.

Emotionality deals not only with what may be within persons but also with what surely is between them. Affect provides a means by which people interact with one another. Fear, anger, joy, love, and care all reflect dispositions toward and responses to other people. If people lived in complete isolation, there would not be the *need* for many of the emotions that people experience and express. Attention is rightfully paid to emotions in the process of educating persons in the community of faith because it is the *community* of faith. People in the church should share the tragedy and trauma of life with one another, as well as its joy and celebrations. The power and meaning of these communal acts will be dependent, at least in part, on individuals who learn how to express and receive the emotions that transcribe human relationships.

Emotions and learning have not always been viewed as directly related. The relationship between learning and emotions is subtle, but I think that learning influences some emotions and that learning is influenced in turn by the feelings, motivations, and inhibitions that people bring to a learning situation.

## Can Emotions Be Learned?

Is it possible that people can learn to love? Can they learn trust? Is human emotionality influenced by learning? These questions are fundamental to learning in the community of faith. There is no secret to the gospel's abiding vision that the people of God are to love God, one another, the stranger outside the community, and even the enemy in their midst. Jesus summarizes the law in terms of loving: that we love God and neighbor and, by inference, ourselves. But do people learn to love?

I feel—"feel" is the appropriate word—very much alone in raising this question. When I consult the writers on whom I most depend and with whom I find myself in most consistent agreement, "affective," "feeling," and "emotive" are not words in the indexes to their books. Perhaps I am skating on thin ice. If others don't mention it, maybe it's not worth mentioning. But something hammers away at me. If the affective elements are important for the life of faith, and most of these writers would agree that they are, why the silence?

One possible reason is that while love is accepted as a central issue in the Christian gospel, it is not construed so much as a human feeling as it is a disciplined set of behaviors by which persons relate to one another. In many ways, I support this characterization of love, especially in a society where love is so frequently perceived in erotic or sentimentalized ways. Love is not just a feeling. It is a way in which one spouse acts toward the other, even when he or she may not feel like acting that way. It is a way in which Christians perceive other people in the world and relate to them. Loving God has far more obedience, reverence, and discipline in it than feelings of euphoria or wholeness. But love does include some feeling, some setting of the heart, some disposition of the self toward the loved one that is more than discipline, more than a set of behaviors, more than thinking. While love is more than human emotion, and is cheapened whenever it is reduced to merely the emotional, it does have its emotional dimensions.

A second reason there is so little mention of love in writings about education in the community of faith may be that an implicit assumption exists that human emotions are not learned. To the extent that love has "feeling" as one of its components, it is a part of the endowment with which human beings come into the world. Infants are born with the capacity for fear, for attachment, for love, for joy—just as they are born with the ability to cry or to grasp.

Such a position is inadequate. The ability to care is really not as much an inborn phenomenon as it is something learned in the midst of life with others. Even if a part of human emotionality is inborn, as it no doubt is, emotions are susceptible to tutoring. For example, people may not learn "to fear," but they do learn what to fear and can learn a variety of responses to make in the presence of their fears. Maybe the readiness to love comes as part of the native endowment of being human, but people can learn how to love well and what to love most.

Thus love has an affective element to it that can be influenced by learning. There are other aspects of emotionality in Christian faith, and they require education as well. The question changes from "Can emotions be learned?" to the contention that affection is crucial to—dare I say at the heart of?—Christian faith.

### Learning Emotions

If emotions are a part of the believing process, and if they are influenced by learning, then responsible education for faith requires some kind of tutoring for human emotions. I want to propose four ways in which appropriate educational intervention can influence and fashion emotionality.

*Naming.* People sometimes require the kind of learning that helps them name or identify their emotions. Very frequently, anger and fear are confused with each other. A response that may be proper for fear—running away from an imminent danger that can be avoided—is a faulty response to anger. Anger is better dealt with by confronting the person who evoked it than by running away. Emotions often have a common signaling mechanism, and it takes some skill to determine which of several sometimes competing emotions is sending the signal. The ancient wisdom of the Hebrews is relevant here. Names do have a power, and if the individual can name the emotion ("I am angry"), there is a better chance to figure out why the emotion has occurred and what should be done with it ("I am upset by your attitude toward me, and we need to talk about it").

*Expressing.* People sometimes need help in learning to express their emotions. Persons can interact with each other in very faulty ways because they do not know how to express the emotions they feel. For example, an individual may be very angry at another person but, instead of expressing anger, acts in the opposite way by expressing affection. The affection is flawed, and the resulting interaction is confusing to both persons. Sometimes people need help to find the appropriate ways to express their feelings. For many people, anger toward God is unconscionable, and they do not know how to express it. As a result, they may express rage against someone else, sometimes in the name of God and for the presumed benefit of God. More than one religious crusade owes part of its origins to someone's unclaimed, and thereby uneducated, anger.

*Disciplining.* Some people need to learn how emotions can be disciplined and channeled. For example, a person may "love" God because of a deep emotional need to be cradled and kept safe. As a result of these interior feelings, the person creates an outward expression of love toward God that consists entirely of enjoying the presence of God. The love, in this case, is misdirected and undisciplined. The person who loves God should express at least a part of that love by caring for the people and world whom God loves.

*Discovering.* Other people need to learn emotions that have not been a part of their lives. Some people have never learned to love. They do not know how to extend care and concern on behalf of others. Some people have never learned about joy. It may not be that their lives have been tragic or sad, they just do not know how to be joyful. These people need to discover the emotions that are fundamental to the vocabulary of faith.

Faith may teach some emotions that are not readily learned in other contexts. For example, I think a sincere faith introduces an emotion that can be called sadness. Christian people live both with a vision of the world as God longs for it to be and with the reality of the world violated by human sinfulness. The resulting feeling is sadness, which is different from a mild form of grief. Grief is a reaction to something that has been lost. Sadness is a reaction to what could be but has never been. Sadness is based on a vision never realized, grief on a reality destroyed. Faith gives people a vision and introduces them, indirectly, to an emotion they may not have felt apart from faith.

Some people need to discover the emotions that arise when they experience being loved. I have talked with more people at church who have difficulty feeling loved than loving others, or feeling accepted than accepting others. Some people have a terrible struggle with the Christian faith because they cannot emotionally embrace the grace of God. They have no problem with the idea of grace. They can rationally accept that God chooses to relate to them in the way of grace. But they cannot emotionally receive the grace of God—they are incapable of feeling the reality of grace—and they walk in faith with a limp.

Loving God engages persons at affective levels. And, like other parts of the human spirit, our affections can benefit from education. The failure of faith communities to tutor human emotions results in a devastating form of ignorance within those communities. The ignorance manifests itself in the inability of some people to deal with love and anger, the ineffectiveness with which people express their care and concern for others, and some faulty patterns of piety and spirituality.

### How Are Emotions Learned?

I have argued, thus far, that faith involves affective dimensions and that emotions can be learned. We have identified some kinds of affective learning. But the question remains: How do people learn emotions? I will appeal to two biblical images for a response to this question.

The first is that we love because God first loved us (see 1 John 4:19). People learn about love by being loved and by loving. Emotions are learned as they are experienced and expressed. It helps when the experience and the expression are accompanied by reflection, but reflection alone will not contribute much to the learning of emotions. Emotions are not learned very well from books or lectures. Learning emotions requires experiential learning. But if an individual must experience an emotion to learn about it, is there any way persons can learn emotions they have not experienced? Yes, and that is why learning in faith occurs best as learning among a community of believers. By loving and caring for others and by experiencing life with them, an individual's experience is broadened. Learning is increased. People learn from the experience of others for whom they care and with whom they share the trauma and celebration of life.

The second biblical image underlies the drama of incarnation. We learn of the love of God, according to 1 John 4, because God's love was made manifest in Jesus Christ (v. 9). We learn about God's passion toward us by seeing that passion embodied in Jesus Christ. We can learn emotions by carefully observing them in the lives of others. As a child I learned about anger from my older brother, who could feel and express it to me in impressive ways. I learned about loyalty by watching a Sunday school teacher persistently care for a wife who became an invalid early in their marriage. I am watching my son, who seems to have a fearless streak in him, learn to fear by observing the things his older sister fears. People can learn about emotions from finding them embodied in others, which once again suggests why the community of faith is the best context for faith-learning.

## Affective Influences on Other Kinds of Learning

There is still another aspect to affective learning. Emotions influence other kinds of learning, such as the acquisition of information. The contributions of humanistic education are instructive at this point. Humanistic, as it is used here, does not refer to secular humanism. Rather, it refers to an approach to teaching and learning that focuses on the feelings and perceptions of the learner instead of focusing on the teacher, or the curriculum design, or the objective content. While humanistic approaches have come under critical scrutiny by segments of the Christian community and, for very different reasons, by educational psychologists, considerable evidence supports the assertion that learning information is facilitated by paying proper attention to the learner's feelings.

Research indicates that certain qualities in teachers and certain approaches to teaching not only are appropriate ways to treat other human beings but also facilitate learning. People learn better from teachers who manifest a basic sense of honesty about themselves. Learning is also increased as the teacher enters in relationship with the learners and exhibits a quality of realness to them. Carl Rogers has argued that "prizing the learner, prizing her feelings, her opinions, her person," accepting another individual as "a separate person, having worth in her own right . . . a belief that this other person is somehow fundamentally trustworthy," will also facilitate learning.[4] Another influence on the learning process is the teacher's empathetic understanding of the learners' world. Learners learn better when a teacher can communicate that he or she knows what the learners' world is like, what traumas they face, and what hopes and fears they experience. These fundamental approaches, when effectively translated into teaching activities that embody them, have been shown to increase the level of learning when compared to more traditional teaching strategies.[5]

Why would these strategies influence learning? One plausible hypothesis is that learning itself has affective dimensions to it. People do not just have computers in their heads to receive, store, recombine, and output information. They also have feelings. They have an internal image of who they are, and they make judgments about whether or not they are good people, capable of learning, able to use the information once it is assimilated. Learners have reactions to the people who help them learn. If they feel the teacher accepts them, prizes them, takes them seriously, understands what the world is like for them, learners are freed to deal with the information in ways they could never have done otherwise. If, on the other hand, information is presented by an individual who is not trustworthy, who seems phony, who is distrusting of the students being taught, the learning will be negatively influenced.

Since some in the Christian community have raised considerable questions about the validity of humanistic approaches to education,[6] a few comments are in order. The first is that empirical evidence supports the contention that person-centered approaches to teaching increase the level of learning for many students. Even if the strategies have a debatable philosophical base, their empirically attested effectiveness must be taken seriously. The second is that the focus, in this discussion, is on the kind of learning that can occur in church and the way people should be treated as learners within the community of faith. When person-centered approaches are brought into the community of faith, where people are being redeemed and transformed by the grace of God, they represent some of the most appropriate ways to relate to learners and facilitate their learning. Church may be the one environment where these approaches have their greatest chance of working.

## Behavioral Learning

Another form of learning in the community of faith is behavioral, and some of the most elementary actions that make corporate worship possible, as well as some of the most sophisticated acts of Christian faith, reflect this kind of learning. Children are not born with the capacity to hand along the offering plate, follow the order of service in the bulletin, sing a hymn, or participate in liturgy. These are learned ways of behaving, and certain methods of teaching help people learn behaviors. Adults do not inherit the ability to teach children in church school, facilitate the work of a committee, or advocate on behalf of oppressed people who have no voice. These are all expressions of faithful behavior that require some learning.

The epistle of James argues for the behavioral element of faith: "Faith apart from works is dead" (James 2:26). Jesus' teaching about judgment is centered almost exclusively on the actions—the behaviors—of people. Those who are invited to enter the kingdom are the people who have clothed the naked, visited the sick and imprisoned, fed the hungry, welcomed the stranger, and given drink to the thirsty. Those who are rejected from the kingdom God has prepared are the people who have failed to do these things (Matt. 25:31–46). Faith is complete only when it has expressed itself as action.

Some Christians would affirm the importance of behavior but resist the argument that behaviors need to be learned. They assume that, if people learn to think the right way about Christian reality, they will in derivative fashion go out and do the right thing.

This assumption is more implicit than explicit, but nonetheless influential. I have heard it in occasional discussions with colleagues at the school where I teach. One person reports on a former student who did academic work very well and had a thoughtful, articulate theology. After some years in ministry, the individual has a serious moral failure or a devastating inability to deal with personal relationships. A promising career is wrecked. In the conversation that follows, I have sometimes heard statements like "I can't believe this person did that, he had such good theology." That statement reflects the assumption that good thinking should produce correspondingly good behavior. Such an assumption implicitly contends that behavior is derivative; it is motivated or generated by some other part of the person. Thus, if an individual can get her mind around the subject, or get his heart in the right place, good behavior will follow. While this may sometimes be true, it is not always the case. I would argue that behavior is as central to faith and personhood as is thought or feeling.

The implications of this position for learning are several. The first is that behavior can be learned. The second is that behaviors *are* learned and are not the automatic outcome of the acquisition of something else. And, third, behavior is as central to what it is to be a human being as are other dimensions. Since faith uses the resources human beings have in their response to God's initiative, behavior is a component of faith, not something derived from faith.

## Learning to Behave in Faithful Acts

How do people learn to behave in faithful acts? One tradition of learning theory, behaviorism, offers an answer to this question. While I reject some of the philosophical assumptions in this theory of learning, its understanding of the process by which people learn behaviors is quite useful. At its simplest level, behavioral learning theory asserts that people learn to do and continue doing those behaviors for which they receive some positive reinforcement; and, conversely, that people stop engaging in behaviors that are associated with negative reinforcement or no reinforcement at all.[7]

*Reinforcement.* Is this true, even in the community of faith? Do people really allow a system of reinforcements to influence or mold their behavior? I think so. Consider, for example, the recruitment of volunteer workers for the Christian education program. In the churches where I have worked, some of the easiest positions to fill have been teachers for adult classes. Some of the hardest positions have been teachers for the younger youth classes. These difficulties may not exist anywhere else, but they have in the congregations in which I have served. Why? One likely explanation can be found in systems of reinforcement that exist in a typical congregation. Adults in a class will frequently thank the teacher for guiding them through the lesson or helping them to see aspects of the text or its meaning for life they had not seen before. The ongoing process of working with adults provides an environment where reinforcements are naturally and readily present. Such positive reinforcements are not as evident with seventh-graders. Their teachers are not likely to get many comments after class about how much the students enjoyed the lesson—even if they did. The teacher is more likely to be greeted by intimidating indicators of boredom or the "I wish I weren't here" attitude some youngsters bring to church school. While many adults have learned to see past these youthful expressions, many others are frustrated and become convinced they are not accomplishing anything.

Having a sense of meaning, making a contribution, being appreciated for energy and skill expended—these are typical positive reinforcement events at church. When they are absent, there is a good chance that people will change their behavior patterns.

Reinforcement patterns are present in churches. Some people tend not to notice them because they have a theology that is skeptical about reinforcements. They think any actions a person takes for positive reinforcement—a kind of reward—is not really an acceptable form of service to God. These people might do well to review the teaching of Jesus. He seemed to be quite comfortable with the idea. The Sermon on the Mount, for example, contains multiple references to rewards. Jesus' words about reward in prayer are instructive:

> When you pray, you must not be like the hypocrites; for they love to stand and pray in the synagogues and at the street corners, that they may be seen. . . . Truly, I say to you, they have received their reward. But when you pray, go into your room and shut the door and pray to your Father who is in secret; and your Father who sees in secret will reward you.
>
> (Matthew 6:5–6)

Notice that the issue is not reward per se. It is the kind of reward individuals seek which determines the integrity of the prayer. To experience the presence and acceptance of God is fundamentally rewarding. To experience the awe of other people because they consider you holy and pious is also reinforcing, but it is ultimately destructive to authentic faith.

Churches would do well to be conscious of the power of positive reinforcement on the learning of behaviors. Whenever a public thank-you is expressed, or an accomplishment noted, or appreciative attention given to individuals, positive reinforcements are present. The theological issue about reinforcement is more related to what behaviors are reinforced than the reality of reinforcements. Congregations must ask themselves: Is what we affirm in this congregation central to the purposes and tasks of the kingdom of God? Or do we affirm those behaviors that are secondary, even peripheral, to the purposes of that kingdom? In terms of Jesus' teaching about prayer, do we create an environment where people learn to pray faithfully alone in their rooms, or do we provide more affirmation to the people who can say eloquent public prayers?

*Modeling.* There are other ways in which people can learn the behavior of faith. An expansion of behavioral theory, social learning theory, has very carefully documented the ways in which people learn apart from specific reinforcing events.[8] For example, people can learn by watching other people. This way of learning can be readily observed in young children. The preschool brother of a school-age sister will notice that she is carrying a Bible to Sunday school and will find a book, any book, and want to take it to church as his "Bible." Or a youth is impressed by a volunteer working with the youth group and begins to adopt the volunteer's mannerisms and typical expressions. People learn behaviors, sometimes even unconsciously, by seeing them in other people, encoding them in their own repertoire of behavior, and acting them out.

Research indicates that the more a learner sees a model as capable, the more the learner will pattern behavior after the model. Likewise, the more the learner has experienced earlier forms of nurturance from the model, and the more the learner perceives himself or herself similar to the model, the more likely the learner is to pattern behavior after the model. In addition, the more models who exhibit a similar pattern of behavior, the more the learner is likely to adopt some form of the observed behavior.[9]

### Behaving to Learn

Behavior, I have been arguing, is learned. It also functions as a teacher. Sometimes, the only way to learn something is to do it. Congregations will organize a mission activity in which young people go to the inner city or to rural poor areas to provide some form of ministry. Frequently, they will return from such trips with a different quality to their faith commitment. The stories they relate to their congregation or parish will reflect sensitivity, concern, and vision that had not been part of their faith before this experience. Acting out their faith has educated them in ways no discussion about it ever could. Daryl Bem, a social psychologist, has argued that frequently beliefs—the cognitive kind—emerge as the explanations people make about their behavior.[10] I do not think this is always the case, but it sometimes is. When people act out love or social concern, or involve themselves in the work of the community of faith, they are likely to grow in ways consistent with their actions. When people engage in action, a part of themselves is put on visible display, and they will see themselves differently.

The ancient wisdom of the church has affirmed this. Spiritual disciplines developed as a way for people to make themselves present to the God who is present to them. They were *disciplines,* however. They consisted of prescribed behavior in which the devout engaged with regularity, intentionality, and consistency, whether they wanted to or not. And, slowly, over time, the behavior created openness in their lives, the presence of God was encountered, and the faithful became what they had been faithfully acting out all along.

## Cognitive Learning

Ideas are not just figments of our imagination. Ideas count. They touch our lives, fill our minds, and influence how we see the world. Ideas are a part of faith, and learning in faith requires cognitive learning.

Loving God with reason is important. The propositions people affirm make a difference in their experience and expression of faith. If someone believes that God is the warrior who calls the faithful to lay down their lives in battle with the infidels, then faith becomes militant, the community of faith becomes an army, and an act of faith becomes war. If someone believes that God is a parent who nurtures, cares, chastens, and guides, then faith becomes gentle, the community of faith becomes a family, and acts of faith become confrontations and care. Doctrine is not neutral, at least for those who take it seriously.

A part of education for faith involves instruction in what

people should think about God and what responses are most appropriate to the God so conceived. Thinking is not the only important or influential dimension of faith. It must occupy its place along with the other two dimensions. But it is no less important than affective or behavioral aspects of faith. Cognitive learning is accomplished by particular learning approaches.

## Cognitive Concept of Learning

The computer provides one image for understanding the processes involved in cognitive learning. At its most fundamental level, and computer takes in information, places it in some kind of storage system, and retrieves the information on command. The information can also be combined with other information that has been previously stored in the computer. Cognitive learning theories construe human learning in similar ways. Information is received by the individual, stored in the memory system, potentially combined with other information already in the system, and retrieved for later use. The ability to store the information and to combine it with other data provides the needed resources for both memory and problem solving. Learning is the process by which events and concepts in the external world are represented in the internal world of a person's thought.

*Information storage and retrieval.* This approach to learning places significant emphasis on the ways in which information enters the storage system. Jerome Bruner, for example, identifies three primary ways in which information from the outside world can enter the individual's internal storage system.[11]

The first is through physical manipulation and action. Instead of using a series of words, the brain seems to be able to receive, store, and retrieve information from muscular actions of the body. For example, the brain uses information in storage learned from previous attempts to catch a ball to give directions to muscles in hands, legs, feet, and arms about the movement necessary to catch an oncoming ball. The whole process depends on very few words. Physical manipulation can also help store other kinds of information. For example, head bowed, hands folded, knees bent are not just postures of prayer. They can help us learn to be prayerful.

A second kind of information storage uses perceptual or sensory images as the method of inputting information. People can, for example, "remember" the smell of bread baking or coffee brewing, or the feel of an infant's soft skin. These sensory events can be so successfully stored in memory that a person can respond to an event as if it were present, even when it is not. If you enjoy freshly baked bread, you can be reading this book, think about the bread, and your mouth will begin to water. You respond to a mental image of hot bread as if it were physically present. In the same way, you can think of the aroma of communion wine and recall the sense of the Presence you felt when you communed with God.

Another means by which information from the outside world can be entered into the storage system is through symbolic apparatus, such as these words. I have certain ideas I want to convey to you. My ideas are represented in words you read, and through the vehicle of the words some form of the ideas will reach your internal system of representation. Once there, these ideas will be compared to other ideas you already have in your memory, and you will come to some conclusion about the truth or error of my ideas. You can also read holy scripture, and a part of the vision that was in the mind of God is conveyed through words to your mind. And if you sense the vision, your life itself can be different.

The process of storage can be combined with different processes of retrieval. Through the symbolic apparatus of notes, for example, the composer writes music that the musician can transform into sounds through some form of muscular activity. In this case, the third kind of information processing (symbolic representation) has been combined with the use of the first form (physical manipulation) to create the opportunity for you to experience the second form (sensory input). When the composer is Bach and the organist is good, the music can move someone in the spirit of worship who neither reads music nor plays a note.

*Facilitating cognitive learning.* These forms of storing and retrieving information can be facilitated in several ways. The ability to use and recall information, for example, seems to be increased when the information is presented in terms of its fundamental structures or basic organizational categories. When one biblical text is encountered with reference to similar texts, or in terms of the narrative flow of the writer, the individual has a better chance of understanding its meaning. Other ways of facilitating learning include arousing the learner's own interest in the material and inviting the learner to voice intuitive hunches about the nature of the information and its relationship to other information.[12] These ways of facilitating learning suggest that the more actively the learner is engaged in the learning process, the greater the chance the information will be stored in ways it can be easily retrieved and combined with other information in problem solving.

## Cognitive Learning and Faith

The processes by which information is stored and retrieved, as well as the strategies which facilitate these processes, are not peculiar to learning for faith. There are some cognitive learning tasks, however, which are. I would like to propose three essential such tasks for people who are learning the way of faith.

The first task is learning the stories of the believing community.[13] A story with integrity and power does not need to be exegeted and exposited to have a shaping influence on the lives of people. Stories do not have magic in them, nor do they engulf people because they are stories. Their power resides in their narrative ability to communicate the faith other people have experienced and sought to express. A story weaves fact and event, feeling and response, past and future into one cloth. The stories of faith are the primordial, fundamentally important content of a faith community. Stories have not only the meaning that is contained in them; they also attract meanings to them from the lives of the hearers. They convey interpretations of previous generations of faithful people and provide a gathering point for the meaning that present life experience brings to people of faith.

A second cognitive learning task is the need to develop a capacity for critical reflection. This ability depends on an information base but requires more than data. It calls for the capacity to manipulate concepts, to reconstruct them, and to evaluate them in light of new information or different experiences.[14] Critical reflection begins with the acceptance of a belief, a doctrine, or a proposition and continues with the ability to hold that concept under scrutiny. This sequence may seem questionable, but I have suggested it because I do not think that faith emerges as people consider all the possibilities and finally arrive at a conclusion.

My daughter has been asking some interesting faith questions lately. Most of them take this form: "How do we know for sure that God exists?" I find myself telling Jenny that we cannot know for sure. Jenny has been nurtured to believe in God. She is beginning, in very elementary ways, to reflect on that belief—to hold it up for scrutiny. She has a belief to work with, however. If she had nothing to hold up for questioning, her task of fashioning faith would be impaired. She has the propositions we have given her, but she must reflect critically on them. If she were to take the propositions we have been encouraging her to believe without any critical reflection, they could never be her affirmations and she would never be freed from either her parents' or her tradition's misconceptions. So, with the risk of error, I will abide by the sequence. People first accept a proposition or a doctrinal statement and then reflect on it critically. The reflection may lead to the acceptance or rejection of a construct, or to its redefinition.

Thinking about beliefs is an activity properly experienced in an environment of humility. Part of what we seek to understand transcends understanding. We reflect and evaluate with tentativeness because we live in the firm grasp of realities that lie beyond our ability convincingly to construct a reasoned truth.

The third form of cognitive learning essential in the way of faith is imagination.[15] The ideas of faith are not just the facts that bind people to an ancient tradition. They also invite a people into the future. The faithful vision of reality has yet to be entirely written. The ideas of faith become part of the ongoing process of the creating God. Imaginative thinking leads people into new paradigms in which faith fashions new experiences and perceptions. Thomas Kuhn, in his classic work on the philosophy of science, notes how scientific paradigms have generally not changed as a result of some new discovery.[16] They have changed because someone saw the existing data in a new way. For example, Copernicus made no new discovery about the relative positions of the earth, the planets, and the sun. Rather, he put the existing data into a new structure, shifting scientific thought from a universe with the earth at its center to a solar system with planets circling the sun. Imaginative faith does not change the creative or redemptive action of God, but it finds fresh meaning in God's activity, new implications, and a revived vision. Imagination joins the visioning capacities of one part of the brain with the rational capacities of another part, resulting in a way of loving God with all the human capacity for thought.

## Learning and Faith

Two points need to be made in drawing this discussion about learning to a close. The first is about an overall learning goal in the community of faith and the second is about the individual nature of learning.

I have spoken about three kinds of learning that relate to three dimensions of faith—affective, behavioral, and cognitive. This separation of the human response to God's initiative is artificial. While it is necessary for the discipline of analysis, my underlying assumption is that human nature is fundamentally unitary. These different ways of learning bring a sense of coherence within the believing person. Because the human unity is multifaceted, providing learning experiences that only nurture a part of that unity gradually bends the individual out of shape. These three approaches to learning are not founded on the idea that people are somehow trinitarian in their makeup and that we must nurture each part to keep these distinct parts from running in different directions, like a team of unbridled horses. On the contrary, they are suggested because humans are, in the image of ancient Hebrews, psychosomatic whole creatures. Body, mind, and feeling are so blended that there is no way to separate them. We must pay attention to them together, in a simultaneous fashion. To go about the tasks of education in ways that only touch a part of what makes us human is inadequate.

The other concern is to restate a point I have already made, but not in the context of learning. People are individuals, and individuals learn in different ways. There is no single teaching approach that will facilitate the same learning in everyone. David Kolb has persuasively demonstrated that different individuals learn with different learning styles.[17] To assume that all people must learn in a particular way is to court a determinism that will surely fail. The approaches to learning discussed in this chapter are more appropriately viewed as possibilities than as prescriptions.

Learning is part of the faithful response to God. It is crucial and necessary to faith, but it is not sufficient. There is more to faith than can be learned. There is the unpredictable movement of God that leaves people convicted of truth. People do not become Christians and grow toward radical obedience to the gospel by learning alone. But there is a call in the Christian tradition to come and learn. Learning helps people know the truth, and learning in the right ways can help them live faithfully as companions with truth.

# 4

# Growing in the Community of Faith

*The years of our lives are threescore and ten,*
  *or even by reason of strength fourscore;*
*yet their span is but toil and trouble;*
  *they are soon gone, and we fly away. . . .*
*So teach us to number our days*
  *that we may get a heart of wisdom.*
                    —Psalm 90:10, 12

Human development is a lifelong drama: birth and first cry, infancy and first smile, toddlerhood and first step, childhood and first day at school, adolescence and first date, adulthood and first job, marriage and first child, mid-life and its successes and failures, later adulthood and its life reflections and last longings. Development does not include all these experiences for everyone, but it does for many. It weaves themes and needs together and balances the future with the past. Even cynical people, in their unguarded moments, sometimes speak of birth as miracle and death as mystery. The saga of human development attracts religious reactions in many people. There is something about it that elicits respect, if not awe.

Few environments showcase human development like church. It provides the setting for ritual commemorations at birth, marriage, parenthood, and even death. Developmental events are frequently reflected in the ministry life of the church as well.

Our Baptist church, for example, has services of dedication for infants. Parents bring their child to the chancel and vow to raise the infant in the community of faith. The congregation then responds with its vow to support the parents in their task and to help with the child's nurture at church. After a prayer of dedication, the pastor takes the infant and walks down the aisle between the pews into the midst of the congregation, saying to the infant, "These people are part of your family of faith." The congregation sits transfixed—six hundred people looking through a hospital nursery window. The infant sometimes coos, sometimes fusses, and sometimes cries. No matter what the infant does, the congregation responds the same, because the infant can do no wrong. The saga of life begins in the midst of congregational blessing.

In September, when the children are promoted to their new Sunday school classes, our congregation meets together in the sanctuary at the beginning of Sunday school. As the first-grade children are dismissed to their new class, they are each given something they are not yet equipped to use, a Bible. These children will learn to read in the first grade, and we want some of their first reading to include a few verses in this special book. The saga continues in the midst of congregational encouragement.

Several times a year, our congregation focuses attention on youth. Two years ago, one young woman spoke during Sunday morning worship and expressed her thanks. She had grown up in our church—blessed at birth, encouraged during childhood, baptized into its fellowship as an early adolescent—and was now preparing to leave for college. She took this time to thank the church, the ministers, her teachers, and other volunteers for the attention she had received and the nurture she had experienced. The congregation listened attentively, and her developmental saga continued with their prayers and hopes for her bright future.

Developmental events are evident in the lives of adults as well. We have a women's group in our church that was formed in the late 1930s. It was originally known as the "brides' class," as the wisdom of that day decreed that young married women should be kept separate from young unmarried women and all women should be educated in faith apart from the men. That class has recently celebrated its fiftieth anniversary. Some of the women who married in their twenties are still members of the class in their seventies. Every Christmas season the members have gathered for an annual banquet. The first banquets were dress-up events for newlywed couples. Then children came, and the Christmas banquet became a Christmas party for entire families. The children grew up, and mid-life shifted the Christmas party back to a banquet again, usually at a restaurant. The class still meets for the Christmas banquet, but now in the church fellowship hall. The room is decorated with care; the table candles shed light on the meal and on the years. There are few husbands still living, and the years have changed the brides' class into the widows' class.

I don't know that any young adult class presently in our congregation will survive for fifty years. Life is too mobile now. Careers are built by moving, not by staying in town. But the women of this class have shared adulthood together: birth pains and parent worries, career successes and failures, hospitalizations and once-in-a-lifetime vacations, the trauma and triumphs of grown-up children, mutual support as each has taken her turn to bury a spouse and re-create the rhythms of life.

In church, more than most other environments, the processes and effects of the developmental journey are on display. The spectacle of people of different ages gathered on Sunday provides one view of development. There is also another view. It is more subtle, but it is there. Every individual at church is in the midst of a personal pilgrimage through life. For each individual, development is focused at a particular point, in a particular place, at a particular time. Take the other morning, for example.

I sat with my young son at the breakfast table. It was a longer and messier time than I had hoped. He had added extra cereal to his bowl. "Jonathan," I asked, "will you eat all that you are putting in the bowl?" "Yes," he promised. My best guess is that we both knew better. After eating three spoonfuls, he darted off to find his older sister or his mother. Before I could get to him to remind him of his promise about the cereal, he had convinced someone that breakfast was over and he would like a piece of gum. I arrived just as the gum was about to enter his mouth. After a series of parental interventions I will not detail here, and which would not withstand the scrutiny of child guidance theory, we were back at the kitchen table, confronted by the bowl of cereal. We negotiated a contract as to how many spoonfuls were required to complete the task successfully and qualify Jonathan for the chewing gum. As we got past the first bite, the bowl "accidentally" spilled. Time was taken for paper-towel cleaning of the kitchen floor. Finally, by what should have been lunchtime, the required spoonfuls had been placed in his mouth and, for the most part, swallowed.

What all was going on in this exchange? Jonathan was developing, and his development was on display. For one thing, he was enjoying his increasing ability to manipulate the physical world around him. Not too many months ago, he didn't have the skills required to get the cereal out of its box and into his bowl. His abilities are growing daily, however, and he takes delight in using them. And something else was happening. Jonathan was discovering that he is a person who is different from other family members, and that he can will life in directions that differ from the way his father wills life to go. Another part of this transaction was fundamentally social. Jonathan has learned that his world has more than one person in it, and that he can convey events to different people in different ways and experience different responses from them.

## Ministry and Development

The evidence of developmental processes can be seen across the faces of a hundred people in a congregation on Sunday morning: old and young, children and parents, teenagers and adults. It is also experienced one person at a time. And in the passing of years, many people evaluate their development in theological terms, just as the psalmist pleaded: "Teach us to number our days that we may get a heart of wisdom" (Ps. 90:12).

People view development through the lenses of a philosophy or theology of human nature, and those lenses influence both what they see and what they conclude. Some people, for example, hold to a version of the doctrine of original sin, which views children as born into the world bent toward sin and in need of protection from themselves. Other perceptions of this same doctrine lead to the assumption that children, if left to their inclinations and given proper encouragement by their world, will follow their natural bent toward the good.

This tendency to view development in the context of both psychological and theological categories is appropriate and necessary for effective ministry. It does create a few problems, however. The first is that a thoughtful perspective must be sensitive to the rigors of both psychological and theological inquiry. Sometimes, a sophisticated use of one is coupled with the naive use of the other, resulting in an inaccurate perspective for ministry. A second problem is that a perspective of development equally sensitive to theology and to psychology may arrive at conclusions that would not be reached on the basis of either discipline alone.

I want to describe development in terms of four models, which in their own ways provide a perspective on development that is both psychologically satisfying and theologically acceptable. The variations in the models do not compete with each other as much as they provide different angles of vision on a complex phenomenon. Once these models are introduced in the context of life at church, I would like to explore them further in light of some broader issues confronting developmental psychology.

## Models of Development

To introduce the models, let's go to the nursery at church. A family is visiting church with two-year-old Peter. As they approach the preschool room, the volunteer worker sees them coming, stoops down to the child's level, and invites him into the room. The child takes one look at the situation, grabs his mother by the legs, and says, "No, no!" The preschool worker says, "We have some exciting things to do and some toys that will be fun to play with." The child buries his head in his mother's skirt and begins to cry. The mother is a little exasperated because this is not the first time Peter has acted this way. When she picks him up to put him in the room, he begins to scream and kick, in addition to being tearful. The preschool worker says to the mother, "It will be all right as soon as he

is in here." But when the mother begins to set him down, he
screams louder. "Don't scream," the mother says, at which
time Peter screams his loudest. The mother is visibly embarrassed and says, "It's just not worth it. I don't want him to grow
up thinking that church is a terrible place. We will wait until
he is a little older and try again."

How can Peter's behavior be explained in terms of his development? What was going on in this incident?

One way of explaining what was happening is that Peter is
experiencing dependency anxiety and is reacting accordingly.
As an infant and young child, Peter learned that he has fundamental needs he cannot meet by himself. While he now has
some ability he did not have at an earlier age, he still feels this
profound sense of dependence on his mother, who gives primary care to him. To be separated from Mother is to be separated from the assurances that fundamental human needs will
be met. Separation creates great anxiety in him. He clings. He
resists being put into an environment that feels threatening.
Peter does what a person under threat does: He tries to reduce
the threat by clinging to his greatest source of security.[1]

Another way of describing this interaction is that Peter, for
one reason or the other, does not want to go into the preschool
room. Any of a number of variables may be the reason: The
last time he was in a child-care center he fell and was hurt, or
his parents had a fight in the car on the way to church and he
fears they may go away, or his mother always does everything
he wants and he has learned that other adults don't always do
things the way he wants them done. Peter has learned that if
he creates enough of a crisis, particularly in public places, his
mother will give in to his demands. So, he screams, grabs,
resists, and protests, all the while knowing—even if only at
some nonconscious level—that there is a good chance that he
will get his way.[2]

Or consider another plausible explanation. As Peter's ability
to think has been growing, his ability to perceive the world and
to make meaning from it has been changing as well. There was
a time, not too long ago, when he could not distinguish himself
from the rest of the world. He was completely incorporated in
parents, environment, and world. It was not possible for him

to identify what was beyond him from what was within him because his mind simply could not handle such concepts. But at two, his ability to think has changed. Peter can now distinguish, although sometimes fuzzily, between what he is and what he has. While he is able to separate himself from a larger external world, he is still embedded in his family and his perceptions.

Peter is changing, and the way his young mind attaches meaning to the world is in the middle of change too. He knows enough to realize the world is not as he once thought it was, but he does not yet know enough to figure out exactly what the world really is like. He is trapped between wanting to be included in family and wanting to find the rest of the world. He may have as much interest in the preschool room as he does in family, and peek into the room at the same time as he is holding on desperately to his mother. Peter is living in the middle of a developmental struggle that is like being inside a cave and looking out. On the one hand, the outside world is full of light and interesting objects. On the other hand, he knows his way around the cave, and it has been a safe environment. He is just emerging from a point in life where, in his two-year-old mind, the cave *was* the world. Now his ability to see through his mind's eye has grown, and he is able to perceive the world as larger than the cave. This sense of offbalance has caught him in this new environment, and he reacts to the tension with a tantrum, an impulsive way of saying he would like to be in the cave and outside the cave at the same time.[3]

Consider one more alternative with me. Peter is not the only person in this incident. And this event has not happened apart from a context. Maybe what happened with Peter is best understood in ecological terms. This young boy is involved in a series of interpersonal interactions. There is an interaction between Peter and the preschool teacher, an interaction between Peter and his mother, and an interaction between the mother and the preschool teacher. The environment also contributes its share of influence to the interaction. Had, for example, Peter and his mother not been at church, the interaction might have been different. His mother might have been less readily embarrassed in another environment. The preschool worker might have responded differently if she were in an environment where she felt more authority to deal with the situation. Both adults may feel a kind of tension in a church environment which they do not feel someplace else. While some dynamic process may be going on inside Peter as a growing two-year-old, he is not developing in isolation.[4]

### Distinguishing Among Models of Development

What are the differences in these four explanations of Peter's behavior at church? The differences are many, but I would propose the primary one is in their respective points of focus. The first explanation focuses on some internal feelings that Peter may be experiencing: his anxiety over separation. The second explanation focuses on Peter's earlier experience, his learning from the past that influences his behavior in the present situation. The third explanation focuses on Peter's cognitive ability, and the kinds of trauma a child may experience as thinking changes—particularly if a function of thinking is to construct meanings of our world and our place in it. The fourth explanation pays attention to the setting, the people, and the context, as well as to whatever may have been going on internally in young Peter.

These four descriptions provide, as a group, some helpful ways of interpreting Peter's behavior in developmental terms. They include a serious consideration of both internal feelings and external contexts as sources of influence. They interpret part of development in terms of learning and another part in terms of internal changes. I do not propose these four models as cafeteria-like options for unreflective choosing. I have proposed them because they provide inclusive ways of viewing human development in the people in church.

## Questions About Development

These models reflect responses to some basic questions a developmental approach must seek to answer. I would like to shift focus, now, from Peter and the church nursery to the larger arena of psychological theory building and to two major questions. The first asks: What most influences human development? The second asks: What happens in the developmental process?

## What Most Influences Human Development?

The longest-standing issue in theories of development has related to this question. Some argue that heredity is the most influential force, and others argue that it is environment.

*Heredity.* The arguments about hereditary influences, at their simplest level, maintain that both physical and psychological characteristics are the result of the individual's genetic endowment. The effects of heredity on appearance and other physical characteristics seem to be beyond debate. But does nature also endow people with psychological tendencies?

Many developmental theorists would answer yes, at least in a general way. They contend that people are born with a genetically determined framework on which psychological development occurs. There will be variations in the way individual characteristics are fashioned, but they will be built on a very similar internal structure. Erik Erikson, for example, theorizes that personality develops according to an epigenetic principle.[5] The individual is born with a built-in psychological sequence in which certain fundamental life issues will emerge in predictable patterns. Like a tulip bulb growing in the spring—with its bladelike leaf first emerging from the ground, then the appearance of a bud, and finally the opening of the flower—psychological aspects of human development proceed according to a ground plan, by a proper sequence, within a proper time.

The more that one argues on behalf of the hereditary influences, the more development can be construed as a gradual unfolding of a biologically based process. Just as genes influence the emerging shape of the adult's appearance, so other genetic influences contribute to the gradual emergence of adult personality.

*Environmental influences.* The other candidate for the dominant influence in the developmental process is the environment. In the 1920s, John B. Watson made the boast, "Give me a baby and I'll make it climb and use its hands. . . . I'll make it a thief, a gunman, or a dope fiend."[6] Whatever influences that were internal to the individual were assumed to be dwarfed by the external influences. Behavioral psychology took Watson's boast and identified an empirically based explanation of the influence of reinforcement systems. In this approach, development is a process by which the organism responds and adjusts to positive and negative reinforcements that are present in the environment. Development thus becomes an ongoing process of learning.[7]

The reinforcement approach, however, is not the only way to consider environmental effects. Environment can also be viewed as a context, or series of systems, in Urie Bronfenbrenner's terms,[8] which influences development. Environment does not control development through contingencies of reinforcement, but it does provide an ecological context in which development occurs. This perspective asks questions about how persons might have developed differently had they grown up in a different place or time.

Recently, an older group prepared and presented a musical at a seminary conference on aging. They shared images, insights, and songs that were part of their lives in this amazing century. They talked about dating in the twenties, trying to launch families in the Great Depression of the thirties, and watching men go to war in the forties while women took jobs in the factories. They reflected on the good times of the fifties and the pain they felt in the sixties, as they watched their grandchildren protest the nation they had fought to preserve. It was a gripping evening and raised the ecological question: How much do historical and cultural events shape adult development? Could these adults be who they are in their mid-seventies if it were not for all these experiences of life? Will elementary children today, who will reach the decade of their seventies in 2050, have a perspective of life like today's seventy-year-olds?

*Interactionist perspective.* This perspective holds that both heredity and environment influence development, and neither alone determines the whole outcome. The models that were proposed in the description of Peter reflect an interactionist perspective. Some influences in Peter's particular developmental crisis were anchored to the heredity processes that resulted in his dependency anxiety and his wanting both to cling to Mother and to enter the nursery. Other influences reflected environmental factors, including the learning he brought with him that day and the ecological setting (the church nursery) where the events transpired.

## What Happens in the Developmental Process?

What is happening in persons that results in development? What processes are at work? These questions attract more than one response, and I will focus on two. Development can be viewed as a process of movement through sequential stages or as a process of learning.

*Sequential stages.* The process of development can be construed as the individual's passage through a series of stages. Jean Piaget's theory of cognitive development is a stage theory.[9] The stages have certain characteristic features. First, the difference between stages is more qualitative than quantitative. The difference, for example, between the thought of a child at six and a teenager at sixteen is not that the youth knows more or can think faster than the child. The adolescent thinks in a different *way,* using a different system of logic. Second, the stages are generally assumed to be invariant in their order of appearance. A child, for example, does not learn symbolic logic before learning to separate internal thought from external reality. The sequence, under conditions of normal development, will not vary. A third characteristic of stage theory is that the stages are assumed to be universal. The stage sequence is anchored in fundamental human structure and occurs among all people, regardless of their cultural setting or the historical period in which they are developing. Cultural expectations or social conditions may influence the development or restrict persons to earlier stages, but, given time and barring major problems, the stages will emerge.

*Development as learning.* A second way to understand development is as an ongoing process of learning.[10] People learn by a variety of processes, and the sum total of all the learning, across time, is development. Thus the difference between a young child and an adolescent is primarily a difference of what has been learned. The adolescent knows far more than the young child, and that knowledge enables the adolescent to live and interact with others in very different ways from the way a child can. Different things may best be learned at different points in life, but the process of development remains, primarily, a process of learning.

*A combined perspective.* The models presented with Peter's case reflect both learning and stage development theory. Peter, I propose, brought a learning history to this situation. He knew what his mother might do if he screamed loud enough and long enough. If his mother acted differently in this situation, and if she continued to act differently, Peter would learn (develop) a different pattern of behavior. Another model suggests that Peter's ability to think was changing, and thereby his ability to perceive himself and his world was also changing. Young Peter was caught in an anxiety-arousing developmental process in which the security of one perception had been disrupted by a more mature perspective.

## Faith, Development, and Ministry

For me, human development is best understood as a function of internal psychological tendencies and external environmental contexts and reinforcements. It involves gradual change within the individual that must be described both in qualitative and quantitative terms. The normal developmental process provides: (1) a learning history that defines the expectations an individual brings to the world; (2) a growing cognitive ability that provides increasingly accurate ways to perceive reality and an enhanced capacity to reflect and interpret events to provide a sense of meaning; (3) an increasingly complex emotionality as perceptions, events, experiences with others, and reflections all interact with each other; and (4) an increasing ability to mediate and interpret behavior. The pace of development quickens and slows at different points in the process, but the process is lifelong.

How do these developmental processes influence the growth or development of faith? For James Fowler, who sees faith as evolved and evolving ways of relating to centers of power and meaning, faith is itself a structural developmental process.[11] For G. Temp Sparkman, faith is a more durable theological reality that is realized in persons' lives through a developmental process.[12] For Dwayne Huebner, faith is remembering God.[13] Memory changes over time, as life experience and the evidences of grace shape its contours. But the change is not developmental in the sense that it conforms to an orderly, predictable pattern. These three positions reflect a range of possibilities: from faith as a developmental phenomenon, to faith influenced by developmental processes, to faith that changes quite apart from developmental events. Which possibility is most appropriate for the concept of faith proposed in chapter 2?

Faith was characterized as an openness to God, as transforming participation in the purposes of God, and as a process of fashioning meaning. How does faith so characterized develop or grow? First of all, it develops as a work of grace. The growth of faith does not occur by either effort or developmental events apart from the ongoing craftsmanship of God. Second, faith develops as persons learn the lessons of faith. As emotions, behavior, and thinking are tutored, faith grows. Third, faith grows as a function of developmental events that reshape an individual's ability to perceive the world and make meaning. This perception cuts across the possibilities mentioned above and begins to set the agenda for ministry.

Attending to human development can become a valuable resource for ministry. If faith itself develops, then a sensitivity to human development will increase an ability to understand faith and minister to people in ways that facilitate its growth.

If faith remains a constant, theological reality in the lives of persons, then a sensitivity to the ways people grow and change will enhance our ability to understand why, over time, they perceive and respond in different ways to faith's presence. If faith grows by learning experiences, then ministry will require appropriate encouragement and strategies for learning opportunities.

Ministry interacts with developmental theory in still another way. As I have characterized development, some aspects are determined, either by external or internal influences, while other aspects remain free and open-ended. How do we minister to people who may be free to develop in some ways but determined to develop in others?

To the extent that the developmental process determines some events, ministry must find ways to deal with people who are controlled by forces beyond the realm of the church and its people to influence. Ministry becomes a means of helping people deal with the consequences of the unavoidable. There is a place for ministry in such environments, of course. A hurricane blows ashore or a tornado tears across the prairie, leaving devastated and pained people in its path. No act of ministry can stop the winds, but a variety of responses are possible to help people in the aftermath.

To the extent that development has more open-ended and less deterministic elements, the work of the community of faith becomes formative as well as restorative. The response of the church will need to be more intentional and more comfortable with complexity. To the extent that development travels a more open-ended path, unique to each developing person, ministry efforts will need to be more individualized and specific.

Taking note of developmental issues is important for the task of understanding people. Attending to development, however, requires paying attention to a moving target. People are changing, and what may have been true of them ten years ago may not be true in the present or the future. Perhaps the most significant outcome of a ministry informed by developmental understanding of people is respect and humility. It reminds us of the complexity and variety of the human creation, which generates respect. It leaves us baffled and troubled by all the variables and all their combinations, which generates humility.

Paying attention to the years of our lives is an ancient tradition for people of faith, as the psalter reminds us. It is also a worthy tradition. So teach us to number our days that we may get a heart of wisdom.

# PART TWO

## Children, Youth, and Adults in the Community of Faith

This book is about paying attention to individuals so the community of faith can help them learn a Christian way in the world and grow toward maturity in faith. Part One addressed the issues of attending to people, the nature of faith, the process of learning, and the movement of human development. Before introducing Part Two, I want briefly to review the perspectives that have been presented so far.

Faith was characterized as an openness to God, as a relational, transforming participation with the people and purposes of God, and as a process of meaning-making. Faith changes over time, as people encounter the events of life and the work of grace, but faith at each point includes these elements. People experience and express their faith in affective, behavioral, and cognitive dimensions.

Learning nurtures the growth of faith. People come into their faith-knowing by grace, to be sure, but also by learning. Learning in faith must address all the dimensions of faith, and so affective, behavioral, and cognitive forms of learning are required. Individuals learn these three dimensions differently, so learning in faith requires a variety of approaches.

Development is a function of both internal psychological tendencies and external environmental contexts and influences. The normal developmental process generates a learning history that influences the expectations a person brings to life experience, an increasing ability to perceive events with accuracy, a changing cognitive ability to reflect on events and make meaning in life, an increasingly complex emotionality, and an increasing ability to mediate and interpret behavior.

Part Two consists of chapters about children, adolescents, and adults. The children get two chapters because I want to invite you to take children seriously and attend to them as people of faith (chapter 5), and because I establish some issues in the discussion of children (chapter 6) that subsequent chapters will address. Adolescents and adults deserve more than one chapter each, but the purpose and limits of the present volume have resulted in one essay about youth (chapter 7) and another about adulthood (chapter 8).

These chapters explore people of different ages in terms of the issues addressed in Part One. My primary concern, in each chapter, is to focus attention on individuals at various points in life with a view toward ministry with those individuals. The information derived from attending should inform life together in the faith community, where people share corporate worship, education, and programs of missions and ministry. Attending to persons is fundamentally important, but it is not enough for effective ministry. Ministry also requires informed and sensitive effort.

Last winter, Jenny came home from her Sunday evening children's education program somewhat withdrawn. When it was time for her to get ready for bed, she left for her room and, in a few minutes, came back crying a frightful cry. She collapsed onto my lap and, between sobs, struggled to ask, "Why, if God made the world and people, would God let there be wars and nuclear weapons?" I held her for a while, which was about the only thing I knew to do in the face of the unanswerable and fear of the unthinkable. After her emotions relaxed, we talked. A television miniseries about a nuclear war was to begin, and that evening's church program was intended to help children deal with the emotions they might experience watching this drama. Jenny's leaders are sensitive and caring and know how to attend to children. Their concern about the effect of this television series showed their sensitivity. This particular ministry effort, however, increased the fears of one third-grader rather than allaying them. There are ways that fearful subjects, like this one, can be addressed with adequate opportunity for closure and emotional debriefing. Sensitive attending is necessary but not sufficient. It must lead to informed expressions of ministry.

The chapters in Part Two attend to the faith and developmental experience of persons. But this attention is in the service of identifying sensitivities and strategies for ministry that help people learn a Christian way in the world and grow toward maturity in their faith.

# 5

# Children of Faith
and the Community of Faith

*In every hour the human race begins. We forget this too easily
in face of the massive fact of past-life, of so-called world history. . . . In spite of everything, in this as in every hour, what
has not been invades the structure of what is, with ten thousand countenances, of which not one has been seen before, with
ten thousand souls still undeveloped but ready to develop—a
creative event if ever there was one, newness rising up, primal
potential might. This potentiality, streaming unconquered,
. . . is the reality child: this phenomenon of uniqueness, which
is more than just begetting and birth, this grace of beginning
again and ever again.*

—Martin Buber

It is easy to sentimentalize childhood and, in the process,
envision a world that never is, relegate children to it, and
thereby make them invisible to the adults who are fashioning
a real world in which children live. Martin Buber, in the words
quoted above, invites us to see children for what they are: our
most intimate link with the future.[1] They are the most embracing evidence of the continuing work of a creative God. They
are altogether human and enjoy whatever entitlements are due
any human. That they are young, that they have more potential
than history, enhances their entitlement rather than diminish-
ing it.

People of faith have tended to respond to the children in
their midst in one of two ways, much like the responses described in the gospel account of Jesus and the children (Matt.
19:13–15). One response has been to keep the children in the

distance. The disciples, worried about the things Jesus was saying and wanting to protect him from the constant barrage of people pursuing him with their pains and threats, kept the children away. Churches' efforts have seldom been blatant, but in a variety of ways they have also kept the children a comfortable distance away. The other response is to include and bless them. Jesus overheard the disciples, interrupted them, and invited the children into his presence. He was in the middle of a theological discussion, according to Matthew, but deemed the children of greater importance than the moment's teaching. Jesus included the children in the middle of an adult world and found a way to bless them. Some individuals and congregations also know how to bless children. Such knowledge is sacred.

Many of the churches I have known have some of both responses in them. They have usually talked a pretty good line on behalf of children. They take good care of their own. They educate, confirm, and seek to win their children to faith. Yet while they invite and nurture on the one hand, there has been, on the other hand, a tendency to build walls that keep children at a distance.

One student's evaluation of the Christian education ministry of a church included this description of the children's Sunday school room: "The room was brightly colored with a mural of Noah, the ark, and the animals painted on the wall. The other walls, however, were mildewed." Floods have always been tough on painted walls! The description presents a contradictory image. The mural was an attempt to create something pleasing for the children, but the mildew suggests a lack of the daily and weekly care that this too-wet room obviously needed.

If parishes and congregations are to include children and care for them, several things must happen. First, the adults must be willing to learn from the children. There are some truths that children teach more persuasively than do any other groups in the community of faith. Second, congregations need to reassess some of their attitudes and practices toward children. Attitudes can exclude children from meaningful involvement at church as effectively as a minimum age limit. Third, adults need to learn how to attend to children. As the American population continues to age, and a growing percentage of adults do not have children living with them, an increasing number of adults need to learn or relearn the basic skills required for attending to children. Finally, adults will best learn from and provide for the children at church as they understand children's experience and expression of faith.

## Learning from the Children

Children are irreplaceable sources for theological insight. I have spoken more than once about my own children in this book. One of the reasons they come so frequently to mind is that I have learned about faith from them in ways I have not learned elsewhere. They do not intend to teach me, and if intentionality is basic to teaching, they are not really teachers. However, they have portrayed life for me in ways that have brought fresh new insight. The day Jenny was born was a day I discovered grace—if not for the first time, at least most convincingly.

It is no secret that grace is crucial to understanding the gospel. The redemptive work of God, the pursuit of God in our lives, the initiative God takes, the eagerness of God to love, the ability of God to love us when we are unlovable—all these are etched into the character of God's grace. I had known about these things, taught them, and preached them. Then, on the day that Jenny was born, I felt them, and the reality of God's grace sank into me in a way I had not previously known.

Jenny came into the world in the afternoon. It had been a long day of labor for my wife. I was there as friend and encourager, but the work and the pain were hers. When Jenny was born, the physician cut the cord and handed her to a nurse, who wiped the stuff of birth from her, wrapped her in a blanket, and brought her in a warming bassinet to my wife and me. I reached out to this new person and felt an incredible rush of love for her. I had loved others: parents who had given me life and raised me, a wife with whom I shared that life. These loves were, in part, a response to the love that had been expressed to me. There is a reciprocal nature to loving parents and spouse. I loved this little girl, however, just because she was.

It was the first time I had ever known a love in me that was not derivative. It was love extended to someone apart from what she did—or ever would do, love which, once fixed in a Minneapolis hospital delivery room, has been amazingly unrelenting.

When I experienced this love in me, I had a new vision about the grace of God. I learned about loving someone who could not return that love. I learned something about longing for relationship with her and wanting what was good for her. In my feeble, inexperienced way, I "graced" Jenny her first day on earth, and the grace of God has never been the same thing to me since.

Children, by their very presence, provide the opportunity for people to experience a part of themselves and a part of the creative love of God. This is not true for all people, of course, and no one is less human if children do not evoke such reactions. But incidences of the galvanizing, insight-generating kind, as in Jenny's birth, are not isolated or uncommon. They are not everyone's experience, but they are the experience of many. Children need the community of faith and the gifts and grace it can share with them. But the community of faith also needs the children and can learn from them too.

If we pay attention to the children, they will raise questions that do not come as readily from other sources. Children ask questions that are not childish. They have a way of stumbling onto the issues that are fundamental to our existence as people related to God and one another: Where did I come from? What is God like? What happens to people when they die? Why are some things bad? Why do bad things happen, like tornadoes and fires? If adults take children's questions seriously, the adults will get a theological education trying to answer them. If the community of faith conscientiously includes the children, their presence will help adults rethink and refeel their own faith experience.

Buber was right. Children are more than "begetting and birth," they manifest the "grace of beginning again and ever again." With each beginning, adults have the unique opportunity to reexperience their own beginning. When the community of faith takes seriously the children in its midst, it has the opportunity to hold a dialogue with the future and, in such dialogue, uncover hope. Hope may not spring eternal, but our vision of what the future can be springs from hope.

## Reassessing Some Attitudes and Practices

The Christian community can learn from the children, but it must also learn to examine some assumptions about the presence of children in congregational life. I do not think churches need more information about children nearly as much as they need to rethink the ways in which they deal with children.

Some congregations appear to operate on the assumption that "normal" worship and life-style is the way married adults worship and live. Variations from the middle adult pattern are seen as abnormal. Some people conclude that children don't know how to behave in worship, young people are disrespectful and rowdy, older people are a little cranky, and single adults have never really settled down. Such attitudes need to be replaced with a broader definition of "normal," which construes a wider range of behavior as typical and appropriate for worship and ministry.

Congregations need to develop the attitude that children belong in their midst, even if they are disruptive at times. They fidget during the sermon and interrupt their parents. They drop the hymnal in the middle of the pastoral prayer. They do the things that make life at church more confusing. If people don't intentionally develop attitudes of inclusion, they may practice exclusion by default.

Congregations also need to rethink some of their attitudes toward the children who are not *in* the church. There is a need for an attitude of discovery as well as inclusion. The children absent from church school are easy not to notice, and children alone in houses and apartments after school are invisible. Congregations have a sacred responsibility to attend to children who have never been exposed to the community of faith.

Children will never pay their way or pull their weight at church. While congregations have been generally accepting of this reality with their own children, patience sometimes wears thin with neighborhood children who disrupt Sunday school because they have seldom attended. Congregations need to reassess their attitudes toward the children who are strangers to the community of faith, who are disruptive when they do show up, or who live with the kinds of exceptionality that make them difficult to fit into the children's ministry program.

Reassessment raises the sometimes painful issue about how inclusive a congregation is willing to be. Many congregations who are disciplined and inclusive toward adults are not sure how to be equally inclusive of children. We became aware of this at my church recently. Some parents at a school for learning-disabled children commented to one of our members about their failure to find appropriate religious education and nurture for their children. They were not very particular about location or denomination, they just wanted to find a congregation where their learning-disabled children could participate. Without knowing it, and without meaning to, congregations had posted an "unwelcome" sign to certain people in the community. It takes special skills, special volunteers, special equipment, and special money to welcome special children. Some congregations have these resources but have not paid attention to the children with special needs in their community.

The process of reassessment is sometimes troubling. Congregations may discover that they don't want children in the church building who will soil the new carpet or disturb worship. We have our ways of asking them to keep quiet, so people can hear the gospel. And our ways with the children sometimes shroud the gospel from our own ears.

As adults deal with their attitudes, it will be important for them to avoid sentimentalizing childhood. Children learn to sin and get as good at sinning as everybody else. Children are no more special than other human beings. Churches need to reassess some of their attitudes toward children simply because they are people whom God loves, who have been invited to the celebration that is the kingdom of God, and who need redemption—just like everyone else who has grown up in the human family. Children don't need a Disney church with a Sesame steeple. They need congregations who will be agents of God's redemptive grace to them and who will include them as participants in the community of faith.

Congregations also need to develop a posture of advocacy on behalf of children and parents. Children cannot raise their own voices in ways that will be heard, and they are not always mature enough to know their needs and name their hurts. Churches can speak on behalf of children, through both corporate efforts and the actions of individual members. Parents need advocates also. The number of families who live away from extended family members, the number of two-career marriages, the number of blended families, and the number of single-parent families mean that today's parents are working with less time and less support from others than were parents in the 1950s. Some of the institutions parents depend on to help with the tasks of value formation, such as schools or agencies serving youth, are themselves strapped by limited resources or legal restraints and do not provide the help they once provided. Churches can pay attention to parents by forms of ministry that nurture family life, that help single parents, and that help children in single-parent families find sponsorship and support from other adults.

The community of faith needs to reconceptualize ministry to families, learn to advocate on behalf of the children, and invest themselves in the public arena on their behalf. The churches of a community are at their best when they remember people who have been forgotten and seek to reconcile people who have been estranged.

## Attending to Children

If individuals learn how to learn from children, if congregations reassess their attitudes and practices with regard to children, then the process of good attention to children has begun. It will continue as adults make other intentional efforts.

For some adults, the ministry of attending requires their learning to treat children in some of the ways they treat adults. For example, some people who readily perceive adults as unique individuals relate to children as if they were all the same. Children are as different as adults and will be misunderstood if they are lumped into one group. Adults must also be willing to listen to a child, which frequently means attending to actions and moods, not just words. Children, like adults, do not always have words for their joys, concerns, or burdens. And although they may not have words, they are frequently more demonstrative than adults with their feelings and tensions.

Paying sensitive attention to children calls for a hermeneutic of respect. Attending involves some interpreting, and a hermeneutic is a guiding principle one uses in the process of interpretation. By a hermeneutic of respect, I mean that adults should avoid belittling the worries and problems children have, take seriously the integrity of the feelings children express, and realize the authenticity of their joy, pain, hurt, and celebration. Children may experience life differently from adults, but their experience is no less intense, no less real, and no less frightening.

Attending to children also requires a commitment to focus on the important aspects and not the more decorative ones. Children make the most delightful observations and do the cutest things. But these are decorative. More fundamental and formative aspects of their personhood lie beneath the delightful cuteness. Many adults pay so much attention to the funny things children say that their more serious words go unheard.

## Children of Faith

These sensitivities and attitudes are nowhere more needed than when considering the faith children express and experience. Children are individuals in faith, just as they are individuals in all other areas of life. Similar experiences of faith must not be mistaken as identical experiences. Different children struggle with different dimensions of faith. Children need to be listened to in matters of faith, as in all other areas of life. The listening must include more than words, because words are frequently the least revealing aspect of faith. The faith of children, as in other areas of their lives, should be interpreted with respect. It is not childish stuff. It is the work of an artisan God.

If you have ever been around a preschooler who sees the

natural world with pure religious imagination, a respect for children's faith will come easily. If you have ever been with a school-age child for whom first communion became a holy moment, a sense of awe will come freely. If you have ever been around children who act out their faith in expressions of ministry, a confidence will come readily.

Children's faith is not unerringly wonderful. It has fault lines and pitfalls, just like the faith adults have. Children's faith is not magically pure. They quickly learn about sin and the shadow side of self. But children can be—are—people of faith.

### Expressing Faith

I want to comment on children and faith in the context of excerpts from conversations I had with two young friends of mine. James and David are growing up in families who take faith and church seriously. I spoke individually with these two boys, first when James was four and David was five, and then four years later when James was eight and David was nine.[2] We talked about God, and prayer, and several other topics that are not included in these excerpts.

Q: What are you doing when you pray?
JAMES (age 4): You thank the Lord.
Q: What else do you do when you pray?
JAMES: Thank Jesus and God, too.
Q: What do you think God is like?
JAMES: I think God is the world.
Q: What else do you know about God?
JAMES: He helps us.
Q: What kinds of things would Jesus help you with?
JAMES: Mow the grass.

Q: What do you think that it means for us to pray?
JAMES (age 8): Thank God for the things he gave us, and the things he created.
Q: If you were to say a prayer tonight, what are some of the things you would say?
JAMES: The things that are on the table, that God created, and some of the things in the day that I needed.

Q: What is God like? How would you describe God?
JAMES: God is helpful; he made our world for us, and he helps people in many ways, and that's all I have to say.
Q: Do you think that God is a man or a woman?
JAMES: No one can see God, so there is no telling.

Q: What kinds of things do you say when you pray?
DAVID (age 5): I say thank you for my food and Jesus.
Q: What does it mean to pray?
DAVID: It makes God and Jesus happy.
Q: What is your favorite Bible story?
DAVID: The story of when Mary and Joseph had baby Jesus.
Q: What are some of the things you remember from that story?
DAVID: I remember that the Wise Men gave baby Jesus presents.

Q: What do you think that it means to pray?
DAVID (age 9): Well, I think it's like a way of letting God know how we feel without just talking to him.
Q: What would you say in a prayer, if it were tonight and you were going to bed?
DAVID: Most of my prayers, I thank God for the good life I have and for not anything bad happening to me or my family, and things like that.
Q: How would you describe God?
DAVID: Well, I would describe God as a loving person, very loving, kind; I think things like that.
Q: What does God look like?
DAVID: Well, I think he looks like practically everything.
Q: What do you mean by that?
DAVID: I mean like he isn't like a man, he's like everything: a woman, a child, everything.

Children do express faith through words, but their verbal expressions may not be the most accurate ones. Verbal descriptions sometimes invite adults to evaluate children's faith in terms of the cognitive abilities children do not yet have, instead of the affective and imaginative abilities they do possess. Children express their faith in actions and feelings, and frequently these provide more accurate cues to their experiences of faith than do their verbalizations. Given these precautions, it is still possible to explore a part of James's and David's experience of faith through words. Their words are not enough, however. Much of who they are as believing persons is best expressed in how they feel and what they do.

## Interpreting Faith Expressions

The perspective on faith that was presented in chapter 2 portrayed faith as having several elements. First of all, it involves an openness to God. Second, faith is a relational, transforming participation in which persons relate to God and seek to identify with the purposes of God. Third, faith is a process of meaning-making by which relationships and events of everyday life are interpreted and given meaning. All these elements can change over time, as the individual changes and grows.

When the faith of children is interpreted in light of this perspective, two implications seem evident. The first is that, if faith changes, then children experience faith differently from older persons. There is ample evidence to conclude that children's experience of faith does differ.[3] The second is that, if faith includes the elements that have been identified, and if children have faith, then they should possess some expression of these elements of faith. I think they do and want to use James's and David's responses to illustrate.

Children do express an openness to God. Sometimes they are more readily open to the divine presence than adults are. If they are taught there is a God, they are not likely to struggle with the possibility that there is no God. If they are taught that God is approachable, they seldom assume God should be avoided. For James at age four, "Jesus helps." He used more sophisticated terms at age eight, but an honest and easy openness to God is present in both conversations. David, at nine, described God as loving and kind.

Children experience faith in relational terms as well. When I asked David about prayer, for example, his description was very relational: Prayer was "a way of letting God know how we feel." Participation in the purposes of God is not as readily evident in a verbal interview as it may be in life. At one point in my conversation with James, however, he said that his favorite part of church was when the children did things like a drama about missions and projects that helped people. I can also tell you that a part of James's childhood genius is his generosity. He is always giving things to others. At an intuitive level, James participates in the purposes he attributes to God as much as any child I have ever known.

Both James and David talk of God and prayer in ways that reflect an imaginative approach to meaning-making. The images both boys use in the second conversations are more tutored than the ones in the first. James shifts from describing God as "the world" to a more logical positivist position: "There is no telling." David describes God as like a man, a woman, a child, "everything." Both boys reflect an increasing awareness of the teaching their families and congregation are sharing with them and a readiness to remake meanings about God.

James and David live with an openness to God. In their perspective, God can be known and related to. As school-age children, they are aware of how they can participate in the purposes of God. They are interested in meanings, and their theological interpretations reflect that interest. They will theologize as life events invite them to or some adult asks them to. James and David are children of faith, and their response to God is drawn from the same elements that other people of faith use.[4]

Children are a gift to the community of faith. When the church takes them seriously, it acknowledges the gift and responds with the gratitude of stewardship. Adults can learn from the children and should responsibly attend to them. Children remind adults about who adults are and what they should become. Children are "a creative event if ever there was one." Jesus knew that. "Suffer little children, and forbid them not, to come unto me; for of such is the kingdom of heaven" (Matt. 19:14, KJV).

# 6

# Paying Attention to Children

I was on an airplane, returning from a meeting, thinking about an earlier draft of this chapter. I had written an accurate description of children, in my opinion, but not a very engaging one. It was a late-afternoon flight, late in the week. The people near me were huddled around their books and briefcases and showed the fatigue of the time. No one was talking with anyone. Then the scene changed.

A young child sitting with his mother stood up, turned around, and began interacting with the people sitting behind him. The woman immediately behind the boy walked her fingers up the back of his seat, and he smiled and giggled in delight. The child looked around and found the man sitting in front of me. He was a graying-at-the-temples, distinguished-looking man, and when the child smiled at him, he waved. The child waved back and smiled with a body wiggle that jostled his mother. The man waved again, and the child laughed out loud. This young boy continued finding individuals and interacting with them in one way or another for twenty minutes.

In this brief time, the child initiated more interpersonal interactions than all the adults on that part of the plane combined. He was the only person who had virtually no language skill, who could not walk, and who didn't even have his own seat. He was also the one who got an anonymous group of tired travelers smiling, waving, relaxing, and even talking with each other about the happy child in front of them.

This child did what I decided my chapter was not doing. He invited people to pay attention to him, to take him seriously, and to enjoy his enjoyment of the world. But to do that, the adults on the plane had to be willing to enter the child's world—walking their fingers, waving, and smiling. Adults can stand back and look at children, see what they are lacking, and analyze it. Or they can attend to children in terms of the genius of childhood. I would like you to consider children on their own terms and pay attention to their world. It isn't easy, though. I know.

As you can tell from what I have already said, this chapter has been written with difficulty. At first, it was difficult because I was thinking about "generic" children rather than individuals. I dealt with that problem by going back through the material with my school-age daughter, Jenny, and my preschool son, Jonathan, in mind. That solved one problem, but it created another. When *my* children became the people behind the descriptions, I could no longer be comfortable as the analyst. I am a parent, convulsively bonded to childhood through my children.

I discovered, in the process of placing words on paper, how intensely I long for Jenny and Jonathan to discover a Christian way in the world. I want our—their—congregation to nurture them and extend both the welcome and inclusion of the gospel. Under these conditions, no sentence was acceptable, no idea was adequate.

I want my children, and all children, to experience ministry that benefits the gospel of grace. Grace will do its work, I know, but I want the community of faith to do its work too. In the middle of these feelings and longings, this chapter has limped along.

I hope, in the process of reading, you will discover the children around you. Jenny and Jonathan are behind the descriptions, but James and David and Sarah and Kelly are in front of them. I will say no more about my feelings, but the longings are here, on every page.

In chapter 5, I hope you felt encouraged to attend to children and to evaluate your assumptions about them. Children are people of faith who can teach us some of faith's most important lessons. In this chapter, I want to discuss some of the developmental events and environments of influence that children experience. This information should aid you in the process of attending. Finally, I would like to address ministry efforts that translate attending to children into expressions of welcome, nurture, and inclusion.

## Developmental Events

Development, as proposed earlier, is best understood as including some elements that have their locus within the growing emotional, behavioral, and cognitive dimensions of the individual and other elements that have their locus in the environments in which people live. This is especially true for children, and each dimension deserves some comment.

### Affective Development

Children are typically quite comfortable with all the emotions they feel. They express emotions readily and can quickly move from anger to joy to sadness to fear. Children are able to apprehend before they can comprehend; they feel things they do not understand; they can feel loved before they are able to understand what it means to be loved.[1] As a result, children tend to be more accurate in their perceptions of emotions than they are in other areas of judgment. A child can be in the presence of grieving adults, for example, sense that some threat exists, and respond in ways appropriate to the prevailing emotional cues, such as with anxiety and fear.

In some ways, children are *best* understood in terms of their affective development. Their emotions define a part of their uniqueness and genius. When children are evaluated in terms of cognitive development, it is easy to see what the children do not have and need to develop. When children are evaluated in terms of their emotional development, however, it is easy to see what children have which, it is hoped, the developmental process will not take away. Children can experience joy over simple things. They can be angry but work through their anger quickly. They can be terribly afraid, and the comfort of others will ease their distress. Many adults would experience far less trauma if they still had some of these emotional abilities.

*Young children.* One way of describing the emotional growth of young children is by viewing the child as emerging from various environments of embeddedness. As children's cognitive development allows them to distinguish the internal world from the external one, they begin seeing themselves as separate from the world of objects or other people. This revised perception of the world evokes feelings of both exhilaration and fear. As young children continue to grow, they become embedded in their impulses and use them as a way of saying, "I am distinct from other people."[2] Impulsive interactions are influenced by children's emotions and frequently express them, too.

*Older children.* Emotions continue to change during the school-age years. Older children have an increasing awareness of the self and the ability to reflect on that awareness. While young children gain self-awareness, they do not have the ability to reflect about the relationship of self to others. The maturing cognitive ability in the school-age child makes it possible for the third- or fourth-grader to identify ways in which he or she is alike and different from other children, to determine which children are liked and not liked by other children, and to identify what it means to be included or excluded in a group. School-age children are embedded in their own needs and interests and will evaluate their interactions with others in terms of how their needs or interests have been met.[3]

Children's perceptions of their own competence or inferiority also influence emotions.[4] School-age children are expected to begin mastering the tools necessary for life. They enter a world of expectations and experience both their own and others' judgments about how well they are doing. Failure, even failure that is more perceived than actual, can lead to a sense of inferiority. For most children, a certain tension exists between their perception of competence and their fear of inferiority. This tension energizes the child's emotions.

The character of some emotions, like fear, changes during school-age years. While the young child frequently expresses fear about imaginary threats, the school-age child has discovered realistic ones: a parent's divorce or death, dangerous weather, burglars who may harm their victims. School-age children also begin to express different kinds of love toward others. It is not altruistic in the sense that mature love is, but it is moving in that direction and away from the very possessive and self-centered love of young childhood.

## Behavioral Development

Behavior changes with age. There is a pattern to this change that can help us attend to children and appreciate their participation in the faith community.

Young children behave impulsively. In some ways, they are slaves to their impulses. They cannot make themselves *not* grab for the cookie or knock over the block tower another child has just completed. This impulsive behavior does not signal meanness or disrespect or anger. It is pure, unmediated behavior. It means nothing more than that young children take delight in doing things—making muscles move and making things happen. They behave for the sheer delight of it. Adults will teach the children that they must not grab the cookie or knock down the other child's tower. And over time, children will learn that behaviors can have meaning. In early childhood, however, behavior is primarily for exploring, for delight, for discovering what can be done and how to do it.

As children grow into school-age years, their behavior is more mediated. They think about their actions and have more control over them, and as a result behavior takes on meaning. School-age children have learned that behavior can convey love, anger, delight, and resentment. As older children behave, they observe the ways people respond to them. Sometimes, they will act in uncharacteristic behavior patterns just to see how others will react. Children know how to play with their behavior and are doing just that when they test parents' patience but stay within the bounds of family rules.

School-age children experiment with behavior. They explore how certain actions feel and what consequences they evoke. Their behavior means something, both to children and to the people trying to attend to them. Children also learn that other people's behavior means something. They cease looking at behavior as just another's action and begin to evaluate it in terms of its possible meaning.

These comments on behavior have obviously blended into reflections about emerging emotions and thinking ability. These three dimensions, after all, do not belong to different parts of the growing child; they are integrated at the most fundamental levels. Behavior cannot be considered in isolation from emotion, and neither without reference to cognitive development.

### Cognitive Development

Cognitive processes change several times during childhood.

*Young children.* As young children develop, they become increasingly capable of separating thought from physical action, determining the permanence of the external world, distinguishing between the perception and reality of an object, and developing a rudimentary form of logic.[5]

The young child learns, over time, to separate thinking from doing. At first, these two are the same for the child. When the three-month-old begins to recognize Mother, for example, the whole body is likely to move. Thought and movement—and emotion, for that matter—are molded into one common response. The child will learn to separate these from each other and, by the age of five, will have concepts in mind and can think an idea apart from acting it out.

The child also develops the increasing capacity to understand the permanence of the external world. At first, "out of sight" is "out of mind." The external world, for an eight-month-old, consists of only those things that can be perceived. The child will eventually discover that the external world exists, even when it is not in view, and parents discover that "out of sight" no longer means "out of mind."

Young children also develop a form of logic, but it is not the logic that older children or adults use. The child reasons from particular to particular, instead of in some inductive or deductive method. The result is that, while children enjoy trying to identify causal relationships, the form of logic they use leads to faulty conclusions.

*Older children.* Thinking undergoes dramatic shifts during the school-age years. Older children are capable of classifying objects and concepts into groups and categories. This ability allows them to learn mathematical concepts and begin using a more adultlike pattern of logic. They grow to reject the magical, free-form thought patterns of young childhood. When a normally developing school-age child is given concrete reality—whether it is real numbers, people, objects, events, or religious facts—the child can organize them, classify them, group them, and segregate them, with good explanations for every operation. In this way, children "operate" on the events in their world in a way that was impossible when they were younger.[6] All this cognitive ability makes it easy for school-age children to learn facts, organize them, and identify events, actions, and people.

The developmental events provide a perspective for attending to children and for nurturing their emerging faith. This perspective is enlarged by identifying some of the environments that influence children.

## Influential Environments

Many environments influence children, including child care and school settings, community friends, and the adults next door. The contexts that provide the most significant influence on children's experience and expressions of faith, however, are family and church, and I want to focus on these two environments.

### Family environment

Family is the most important single environment in the life of children. The ancient Hebrews had a sense of this reality. The central teaching of the Old Testament is the shema, "Hear, O Israel: The LORD our God is one LORD; and you shall love the LORD your God with all your heart, and with all your soul, and with all your might" (Deut. 6:4–5). In the verses that follow, instructions for the teaching of this central doctrine are presented. "And you shall teach them diligently to your children, and shall talk of them when you sit in your house" (Deut. 6:7). The family is a crucial environment for the formation of faith and religious understanding in children's lives. James Fowler argues that the young child is influenced in profound ways by the moods and actions of primal adults[7]— those persons on whom the child has a sense of dependence for nurture and care. Although the family begins to lose some of its influence as children grow through school-age years, parents remain the most influential agents for the understanding of values, appropriate behavior, and the importance of religion in children's lives.

How do parents and other family members influence faith formation in children? Or, perhaps more realistically, how can they help children fashion faith?

One way is for parents to pay attention to the religious questions their children ask. Although this sounds like an easy enough task, many parents discover otherwise. The difficulty lies in two areas. The first is that children often ask overwhelming questions, and the second is that the questions are frequently asked in disguise. Children, in my experience, ask questions like "If I get hurt, won't God make me well?" "What happens to us when we die?" "Why did God let the tornado come and blow away Grandma's house?" Children ask questions that adults find difficult to answer, and it is easy for the parent to say, "Don't worry about those things." The child, however, needs an answer, although not the same theological answer adults seek for these questions. A young child needs assurances: that God is not a great punisher perched in the sky to pounce on wrongdoers, and that Mommy and Daddy will do their best to take care of the child. The questions that come in disguise call on parents to hear without over-hearing—without reading into the child's question more than is really there. Children sometimes ask, "Does God love me?" and they are really looking for assurance that Mom and Dad love them. When they ask "Does God get angry at me?" they may really be asking about parents' anger toward each other, or toward a brother or sister, or toward them.

Parents can also facilitate the religious development of their children by faithful actions. Children need to learn to pray, but to do this they need to see and hear their parents' praying. Children benefit from being taken to church, but they will benefit even more by observing parental participation at church. When parents are disciplined in their own exercise of faith, the children will get a clear message about the place and importance of faith in their families.

Parents do not need to worry about "forcing" their faith on children. Decisions about one's own faithfulness later in life are best made from the context of having been exposed to faith, not kept in a vacuum where religious affirmations were avoided. In fact, when parents avoid affirmation or involvement in the Christian community, the child concludes that these are unimportant life issues. While parents' faith will never be adequate for the child later in life, it is an appropriate first lesson.

Children also benefit from hearing their parents share the biblical story. I want to say several things about story later, but the point for now is simply the importance of hearing the Bible's stories from parents. The children will never understand all that the stories convey, but they will conclude that the stories are important if their parents tell them with conviction.

This is an age where the American public looks to specialists for a variety of resources. There is an implicit cultural assumption, particularly among more educated young parents, that good parenting involves getting their children to the proper experts at the proper times. Children do need many specialists, but no other adult can influence a child's religious vision of the world more than a parent. Faith is one area of life where no one is more expert or capable of helping children than their parents. The ancient Hebrews were right: "Teach [the words] diligently to your children, and . . . talk of them when you sit in your house, . . . write them on the doorposts of your house, and on your gates" (Deut. 6:7, 9).

So much has been said about the power of peers, media, schools, and other sources of influence in the lives of growing children that some parents assume they have little or no ability to influence and instruct their own children. This is simply not true. Most children view their parents as authorities, particularly in areas of morals and faith.

## Church Environment

Another environment of influence on children's faith is the community of believers who gather in local parishes and congregations. Children have little sense of church apart from people, buildings, and events. There is no church universal, no sense of participation with a wider communion, just the particular people who gather in a particular place and do particular things. Congregations contribute to a young child's sense of God (1) by meeting the child's basic needs, including space that is clean and safe, (2) by the love and acceptance of the volunteers who work with children, and (3) by a pervasive sense of welcome. "Welcome" may be the most important ministry a congregation can extend the young child.[8] It is something children can feel, even when they are not able to name it. In an increasingly adult-oriented society, there is a crucial need for church environments to welcome children.

The local congregation or parish becomes increasingly influential as the child grows into school-age years. Older children are more aware of the world beyond the family, and the community of faith takes on enhanced power. Churches cannot use their power to coerce and should not use their power by taking the children for granted. Rather, they should intentionally reflect a clear image and vision of the gospel by sharing the Christian story through their words and in their corporate deeds. School-age children require more than a sense of welcome. They need assurances that they do indeed belong within the faith community.[9] Belonging is communicated in no better way than in thoughtful, informed ministry with children.

## Ministry with Children

Most congregations and parishes have children in them. The children have a sense of faith and are open to learning the lessons faith teaches. They will feel the congregation's sense of welcome and want to belong to the community of faith. They will learn and mature in their experience of faith. But how do they learn? What should they learn? How can congregations minister to children?

The questions are best addressed with a reminder from theologian William Hendricks: There is no special gospel or theology for children. The Bible does not have a worldview in which it addresses some things to children and other things to adults. On the contrary, it has a unitary view of the human family. All the people need all of the gospel.[10] The church's ministry should provide young children with those images of the gospel they can most readily understand and share its message in ways that do not have to be rescinded when the children are older. The Christian story needs to be taught to children in ways that do not require reteaching later. Hendricks's answer to the question "How do you speak to a child about God?" provides a sensitive beginning for this discussion. "Very simply and very kindly," he responds. "You must speak simply so the child can understand. You must speak kindly so the child will want to understand."[11]

The answers to the questions that inform a ministry with children differ for young children and school-age children, so this section is divided into two parts. The first deals with ministry and young children and the second with ministry and school-age children.

### Young Children

What can young children learn? They can learn several fundamentally important theological themes. Children's learning should not be confined to learning "children's lessons." Rather, children need to be taught those particular lessons that all Christians should learn and that young children can learn. The first is that God has made the world. Children's sense of wonder about the physical world can teach them about a God who creates and about our human task of sharing in the stewardship of that creation. The second lesson children can learn is that God is love. They can learn that loving acts and kind deeds are the work of God in this world, whoever may do them or wherever they may be done. Children can also learn that God loves them. It is easy for them to accept God's love, perhaps easier now than at any other point in life. Children can also learn that they have friends at church. One- and two-year-olds do not understand the presence of other people very well and do not play interactively with each other. But during the years of young childhood, they learn about the presence of others; they discover and claim friends and thereby begin learning the rudimentary fabric of Christian community.

How do young children learn? They learn—like older children, teenagers, and adults learn—in three ways. Young children learn cognitively. Children ask the classic mythic questions: "Why are we here? Where did we come from? Where are we going?" And the Bible is full of stories that answer mythic questions. Children take delight in well-told stories and will learn the story in terms of its details and descriptions. Young children also learn in affective ways. They will "feel" their way toward understanding. They will learn as much about the gospel by being loved as they will by hearing the story that God loves them. They will learn from the acceptance, welcome, and affirmation they receive at church about a God who accepts and celebrates them. A third way in which young children learn is through behavior. They learn by doing. They will learn about Jesus, for example, by eating the kinds of food that Jesus ate, dressing like Jesus dressed, and doing the things that boys and girls did in the presence of Jesus. They will learn about the God of creation by collecting rocks, twigs, leaves, and grasshoppers. Young children do a lot of things, but they do nothing for very long. They learn best when they are encouraged to learn at their natural energy level—brief periods of concentrated attention across a variety of topics and activities.

A mistake churches frequently make is assuming that young children cannot learn about religious reality. The result of the misperception is that churches provide baby-sitting services and nothing more. When this happens, the children learn very little, but not because they can't learn. The reason is the congregation's failure to accept responsibility for teaching them.

Another mistake congregations sometimes make is assuming that children are not being taught if they are not regimented in chairs, hearing Bible lessons, and leaving the Sunday school room with a Bible verse on their lips. Teaching young children in ways that are foreign and difficult for them to manage is no improvement over baby-sitting.

How can congregations best minister with young children? Among the most important expressions of ministry is the support, encouragement, and training of parents to nurture their children in faith. Even if young children were at church five days a week, staff and volunteers still could not do what parents who accept some responsibility for their children's religious nurture can do. While the church environment is formative and influential, it has less power than the family environment. Another important expression of ministry is the acceptance and welcome children receive within the community of faith. The welcome needs to be symbolized for adults in ritual celebrations, such as baptism and dedication, and expressed to the children explicitly and concretely. Churches also minister with young children as they provide volunteers who are warm and embracing and who are committed to working with children as an expression of their own Christian discipleship.

### School-age Children

As children grow older, their ability to perceive the world changes, their way of thinking matures, their experience with peers and adults widens, they become more reflective and intentional in the way they behave, and they feel differently about themselves and their world. All these changes contribute to the emerging ways children experience and express faith. They also dictate the need for an expanding approach to ministry.

Ministry with school-age children should nurture the growth and development of faith and provide opportunities for the affective, behavioral, and cognitive learning that faith requires. This ministry, however, must be placed squarely within the character and activity of the faith community. Christian faith is not nurtured apart from relational involvement with other people, nor is Christianity a religion for individuals alone. It is concerned with the corporate responsibility and efforts of the church to express the gospel of Christ in word and deed. Ministry that nurtures the faith of children occurs as the children share in the tasks and responsibilities of the community of faith.

John Westerhoff has identified several areas that are both important for learning and central to the life of the community of faith. These dimensions include the *worship life* of the community, with its liturgy and repetitive symbolic actions that express the community's sacred story; the *moral life,* which expresses the community's ethical norms and prescribes ways in which people of faith make decisions in particular moral situations; the *spiritual life,* which focuses on prayer and devotion and the ways in which people live in relationship to God; the *pastoral life,* which invites people to live as neighbors and learn the art and skill of caring for one another; and the *catechetical life,* in which learning is construed as the process by which people reflect on their experience in the faith community in light of the community's tradition and vision.[12] These areas of practical theology provide a way of conceptualizing ministry that helps school-age children learn and that also incorporates them into the mission and worship of the community.

*Worship life.* Congregations begin their ministry with older children—and sometimes determine not to minister to them—in the way they invite children to participate in the worship life of the church. I think that school-age children can worship with the community of faith and that worship provides an important contribution to their learning of faith. However, if they are to be included in worship, children have some learning to do, and adults have some commitments to make.

Children need to learn the skills that empower them to participate as part of the worshiping community. Children do not reach some developmental stage where they will automatically want to participate in worship or know how to do so. They need to learn how to worship, and the community of faith must provide them with the opportunity to learn through participation.

Some of the skills are very basic, like learning how to follow the order of worship and how to respond in prayers and liturgy. As soon as children learn to read, they can participate in these aspects of the service. Children can also learn to sing hymns. Children's choirs can help children learn to worship by teaching both general musical skills and the hymns that are sung in worship. Most hymns are not written for children and contain theology that children may not yet understand. But children can learn to sing them and thereby participate in worship.

Other skills are more subtle. Children need to learn to be quiet and, at times, find something to do in those moments when the sermon does not relate to them or is beyond their ability to comprehend. Being quiet at church does not come naturally to most children, but neither does eating with a fork or saying "please."

Adults must be willing to make some commitments if children are to share in the worship life of the community. Children, after all, do create an intrusion, and these intrusions sometimes lead to children's programming that keeps them out of corporate worship. A number of reasons for excluding children from worship relate to the convenience of parents and other adults. It gives the parents a break from the strain of child-rearing and assures other adults that their worship will be uninterrupted by the needs of children. However, the teaching of Jesus, the mission of the church, and the nature of a community of faith all argue more for the effort required for including children than the convenience provided by excluding them.

As a parent, I sometimes forfeit a part of my worship experience to pay attention to my daughter sitting beside me. I feel the distraction. I need worship, but sometimes I end up parenting more than worshiping. These intrusions on my worship life, however, are merely congruent with the rest of my life, where the demands of good parenting have intruded into my civilized adult world: getting up in the middle of the night with a scared or sick child; forsaking quiet family meals as children learn to eat amid protests, noise, and occasional food fights. I tolerate the intrusion on meals because eating is important, must be learned, and parents must share in the teaching. I tolerate the middle-of-the-night invasions of my sleep because children sometimes need comfort and attention, and parents are the primary care-givers. If I want my children to discover the God of grace and learn to participate in the community of faith, I need to accept some interruptions of my worship. As an adult and as a Christian, how could I want less for any other children?

School-age children can also begin learning the meaning of the elements of worship. They can learn part of the Christian community's story through worship. The sacrifice of praise to God teaches something about what Christians think about God. Prayers of confession and forgiveness teach about human failure and God's grace. The reading of scripture teaches about one of the ways in which God reveals God's self. There are other elements—baptism, communion, sermon, offering—and children can learn not only how to participate in these events but also what they mean and how they reenact the Christian drama of God's reaching and human responding.

*Moral life.* School-age children develop an interest in moral issues that is different from the one they had in young childhood. Their cognitive abilities make it possible for them to categorize, and right and wrong are major mythic categories. The children are not yet able to argue the abstract rationale for the rightness or wrongness of some deed, but they are able to learn a faith community's prescription of right and wrong.

Children's moralizations tend to have an artificial rigidity. Children do not readily distinguish between shades of moral meaning or the influence of contextual events on moral outcomes. Right is right and wrong is wrong. As the community of faith introduces children to moral categories, it should be sensitive both to the rigidity in children's thought and to the ambiguities later life will present. Teaching should be conducted in ways that do not have to be renounced when children learn more mature forms of moral discourse.

School-age children can deal with the issues of personal right and wrong as well as with social moral dimensions. They will learn by watching the moral stands adults take and the community's corporate address of moral issues.

*Spiritual life.* The Christian tradition is rich with resources for prayer and devotion, and school-age children are just the right age to begin learning this tradition. Children can learn some of the classic expressions of prayer, as well as the acceptability of their own individual prayers. They can be encouraged to pray. They can learn about the nature of prayer and about the presence of God that is known through prayer.

School-age years are a good time for children to learn the skills necessary to use the Bible and prayer book or other liturgical resources. The Bible is old enough that it does not conform to most of the characteristics of other books children read and use. If the Bible is to become a tool for devotion, children need to learn how to find references, how to interpret abbreviations, and which parts of scripture may be most profitable for them to read. The Bible was written for ancient and modern people who share a faith tradition, and as children are gradually incorporated into this tradition they can share a part of the biblical story.

Children can learn the disciplines by which Christian people have sought to make themselves available to God and can experience some of those disciplines. Children will not have an adult spiritual life, but they are entitled to explore the spirituality they can experience with the guidance and support of their community of faith.

*Pastoral life.* Several years ago, my wife was teaching elementary children in Bible school. The children spent part of the week making games for younger children, and at the end of the week the class took their completed projects across the street to a children's home and gave them to the children there. By this action, the children in the Bible school class had opportunity to participate in the authentic pastoral life of the church.

Several months ago, I asked my daughter what events she most enjoyed at church. Her first choice was the group she participates in that is primarily organized around mission projects. This year, they have visited elderly and homebound members of the congregation, written persons who had particular needs or were hospitalized, and prepared a play for a church-wide mission emphasis. In a variety of ways, these children have had the opportunity to participate in the pastoral life of the congregation. They acted on behalf of the congregation to benefit others in the community of faith.

These actions of children are sometimes ridiculed. Children singing to old people at a nursing home is a much maligned image of Christian service. My hunch is that the negativity reveals a latent ageism, as well as a misunderstanding both of the ability of children to contribute and of the readiness of older people to receive their ministry.

As children are invited to participate in the pastoral life of the congregation, adults need to be sensitive to the kinds of environments in which children can make a contribution, prepare the children for service in those environments, and respond appropriately to their apprehensions and discomfort.

*Catechetical life.* Children learn about faith in each of the four areas that have just been discussed. There are, in addition, those explicit efforts of the community of faith to inform persons in the way of faith. Westerhoff includes in the catechetical dimension both the process of formation, by which people are incorporated into the Christian community, and education, by which people are instructed in the doctrines and tradition of the community. The children at church present agenda for each of these two processes.

The process of formation, particularly the method of inaugurating people into the community of faith, varies widely among denominations. Protestant families can be divided into those groups who baptize children as infants and later confirm them into the community of faith, those who invite children to make a commitment of faith at their own initiative, and those who do a little of both. None of these approaches is without problems. For example, in confirming traditions, the community of faith takes the initiative to determine when persons are formally invited to confirmed membership in the faith community. Since the initiative is with the church, issues about the exclusion of children from the ritual life of the church, such as communion, become points of concern. In those evangelical traditions that invite children to make their own profession of faith, there is disagreement about the nature of conversion in the lives of children and the age at which children are old enough to make their "decision."

Regardless of the method of inclusion and the issues that attend it, the most significant concern is children's rights to participate in the community's life, to continue to experience the welcome they were extended earlier, and to discover a sense of belongingness.

The processes of instruction should include the telling of major parts of the biblical story and the sharing of the particular stories that represent denominational traditions. Children can begin to understand, for the first time, some doctrinal affirmations and thereby learn some of the content the community of faith holds dear.

Telling the biblical story is a powerful form of instruction. It is the most ancient of ways to convey religious reality, and among the most effective. Stories inform, move, engage, and evoke imagination. Stories place doctrinal affirmations in the context of people's lives as dramatic events. The story's characters and plot inform the doctrine the story conveys, and the doctrine transforms actions and events into an interpretation of people and their God.

Telling the story is enhanced by the development of some skills and sensitivities. The storyteller should be someone who lives into and out of the story. Instruction in faith is not passing on information so much as it is passing on faith. If the story means nothing to the teller, children will usually pick up on that. Iris Cully reminds teachers to be faithful to the text as they retell the story and to pay attention to the way the child will identify with the story.[13]

Children will tend to identify with the circumstances and characters they perceive most similar to themselves. They will identify with Jesus, for example, as the boy in the temple more than with his parents. They will identify with baby Moses or his sister more than with Moses' mother or the Egyptian princess. Some stories may be misheard by children because of this process of identification. When Abraham takes Isaac up the mountain, the biblical text focuses on Abraham and his response to this troubling command to sacrifice his son. Children tend to identify with Isaac and miss the thrust of the narrative. Children need to hear the entire biblical story, but it must be told with a sensitivity to children's process of identification and their ability to hear the story's intent.

Children also learn in instructional settings by activity, not just by listening. Making things that represent the story, acting out stories, researching issues—all these are appropriate forms of instruction with school-age children. The activity must be related to the content by reflection and connection. Doing a project does not, by itself, ever mean the child will connect the picture or craft with the details and implications of the story. Both the activity and the reflection are necessary. Two misconceptions seem to persist in church instructional events with school-age children: The first is to assume they are not learning unless they are listening to someone tell a Bible story, and the second is to assume they are not learning if they are not busy making something. Children may not be learning in either situation. Children learn best when they are able to hear and act and are helped to make a connection between what they have heard and done.

### Faith, Ministry, and Children

This whole section on ministry with children reflects the conviction that children do not just learn during the church school hour. They learn in that setting, but they also learn in worship, in mission and ministry groups, and by participating in the life of the community of faith.

Learning that nurtures faith involves cognitive forms of learning. These include hearing the biblical story, learning doctrinal affirmations and denominational traditions, developing skills to use the Bible and prayer book or hymnal, and learning categories of right and wrong.

Learning that nurtures faith also requires affective forms of learning. Participating in worship and community events, hearing stories in ways that invite the listening of the heart as well as the head, and experiencing both welcome and belonging within the faith community—each of these involves affective learning.

Faith is also nurtured by behavioral forms of learning such as engaging in missions and ministry actions, active approaches to information processing, engaging in appropriate spiritual disciplines, and sharing in corporate moral actions of the faith community.

Faith is influenced by the kind of ministries that have been described in this chapter. Activities such as participating in worship and spiritual disciplines facilitate an openness to the presence and initiative of God. Participating in formational and instructional events helps children relate to the people of the faith community. As children hear the stories of faith and are invited to reflect on them imaginatively, they will have opportunity to fashion meaning.

Children, in their own authentic way, are believing people. Their particular needs are important to the community of faith and are as crucial to meet as any other needs that community encounters. Children do not just learn children's stories, they learn the Christian story. They will learn it best if they are taken seriously, told simply, and treated kindly.

# 7

# Paying Attention to Youth

*The dream begins to fade*
*slowly at first and, with it, hope*
*grows weak and loses faith*
*in a world struggling to grasp a rope,*
*a rope invisible to those who dare to open their eyes*
*in vain attempts to find*
*the imaginary string and then they realize*
*it exists only in their mind.*
*The dream of love is almost gone*
*and one is suddenly thrust*
*face to face with the inevitable question,*
*how to survive without trust?*
*And what can life possibly mean*
*until once again one enters another dream?*
                                        —Andrea Pollard, 1987

*Our ministers, long time by word and pen,*
*Dealt with them, counting them not boys but men:*
*Thunderbolts they shot at them, and their toys:*
*But hurt them not, 'cause they were girls and boys.*
                                        —John Bunyan, 1686

Andrea's poem struck me. It conveyed her meaning, but as she read it during a youth-led worship service, it took on another meaning for me. It became an image of adolescence, and I began thinking about young people I have known at church. They have had some dreams dissipate. Forsaken in a romance, betrayed by friends, excluded by a peer group, cut from the team—most of them collect broken dreams as they grow through adolescence.

For most young people, just as Andrea suggests, when one dream disintegrates, another begins to take shape, sometimes better than the one it replaces. Dreams lend meaning and have a way of guiding adolescents toward the adult world. The dreams of youth help envision a future and focus on a place in it. A romantic dream between two young people takes them into some unspoken future when they will share life and love, work and wealth. When the romance breaks up, the hurt comes not only from pain of abandonment but also from the crisis of a broken dream. Usually, there will be another love, and the dream will emerge once again.

Adolescents struggle, in Andrea's words, "with the inevitable question, how to survive without trust?" The world they perceived as children is not what they thought it was. New expressions of reality dawn on them, and they greet the newness with external excitement and internal worry. They embrace the new but fear surrendering the old. Adolescence is a membrane, and both childlike and adultlike images of the world pass back and forth through it. For many, "how to survive" is a baffling question.

Adults are sometimes baffled as well. Who are adolescents? In American society, they are perceived as no longer enough like children to be treated as children, but not yet enough like adults to be treated as adults. So, in John Bunyan's verse, adults might shoot thunderbolts at them and their toys, but they would "hurt them not, 'cause they were girls and boys."

Adolescence is not just a time of struggle, storm, and stress. It can also be a time of intense and rich life experience. I recently read an interview with a parochial high school junior. When asked, "Have you ever had any moments of ecstasy?" This high-schooler replied, "Yes, being an altar boy at midnight Christmas Eve mass, the healing of John [his younger brother], and slow dancing at the prom." When faith and love go well, they can go very well. There is joy, insight, and even ecstasy in some adolescent days—and nights.

Dreams that form and fade and are fashioned anew. Struggles that come with threatening potential and go, usually leav-

ing only minor damage. Questions that haunt the adults who
live with and care for young people, and answers that emerge
from love's persistence. Meaning that comes in the encounter
of God's presence, and in the embrace of young love. Adolescence is full of nouns and clauses looking for verbs and predi-
cates. It is an era that raises absorbing questions about being,
even though the days are stuffed full of doing.

Teenage persons, like children and adults, deserve careful
attention and thoughtful expression of ministry so they too can
learn a Christian way in the world and grow toward maturity
in faith. Our concern is about all youth, of course, but picture
with me some young people at church.

Recently, I returned to a congregation I had served some
years ago for a "youth emphasis." The youth choir sang for the
service and, at the proper time, moved from the pews to the
chancel. The singers were clothed from knee to neck in choir-
robe blue—and from knee to toe in athletic socks and Reeboks
or black high-tops. They sang the anthem, and I began to speak.
I doubt if they will remember what I said, but I will never forget
the picture of adolescence they composed. They were American youth at church: dreaming and struggling, baffled by life's
perplexity, and ecstatically sure about life's goodness.

This chapter invites your attention to youth. First, I want to
attempt a characterization, if not a definition, of adolescence.
The need for such an effort may tell you, already, that adolescence and childhood are different developmental eras. Second,
I want to identify some of the developmental issues adolescents
confront and, third, examine some of the environments of
influence in their lives. A sensitivity to these issues should
facilitate attending to their experience and expression of faith,
and attending to the faith should provide the appropriate context for evaluating youth ministry.

## What Is Adolescence?

The further people move through the developmental journey, the more cultural expectations influence that process. In
young childhood, a task like learning to walk is influenced
primarily by the physiological maturing that makes walking

possible. In adolescence, however, major developmental events are most influenced by social values. Teenagers learn about male and female roles and about occupational and educational expectations. Even the physical changes that occur in adolescence—growth toward adult shapes and strengths— have significant developmental impact in terms of the cultural values associated with those bodily changes.

Adolescence, probably more than any other stage of life, varies according to the culture in which the teenage person lives. Adolescence itself is far more a cultural invention than it is the consequence of some physiological or psychological programming. And as a cultural invention it is a relatively recent phenomenon. One hundred years ago in the United States, adolescence did not exist in its present form. In the 1880s, sixteen-year-olds were more likely to be working in the mill or on the farm than attending school, were treated as adults, not juveniles, when they were accused of crimes, and were expected to function in society in more adultlike than childlike ways.[1]

Other cultures treat teenage persons very differently from the way they are treated in contemporary America. For example, some cultures ceremonially pass persons from older childhood directly into the novice stages of adulthood. When children in these cultures reach a certain age, they are considered adults, removed from the special patterns of treatment extended to children, and incorporated into adult expectations and roles. Still other cultures distinguish between youth and childhood but do not grant teenagers the options and choices typically available to American youth. They require teenage persons to abide by a set of rigid cultural rules and accept the decisions their parents make regarding occupation and spouse.

Because adolescence is so heavily influenced by culture, it is difficult to define. It is not just a group of years in the human life cycle, such as ages thirteen to eighteen. Both its beginning and ending are elusive. Typically, adolescence in America is assumed to begin with the physiological changes that result in puberty, usually between the ages of eleven and fifteen, and to end when the individual is able to function in roles associated with adulthood, including a certain psychological independence from parents and the ability to be self-supporting.[2] By these criteria, some people never leave adolescence! Or they live, like many college or graduate students, in the tension between being psychologically independent but financially dependent.

Perhaps the best way to define adolescence is by examining some of the developmental events that young people encounter.

## Developmental Events

While the American phenomenon of adolescence is deeply embedded in cultural needs and expectations, major shifts in emotional, behavioral, and cognitive development occur during these years. In fact, the pace of development that slowed during school-age childhood quickens during the teenage years. The faster pace of development, especially noticeable in physical growth, is indicative of the changes occurring in other areas as well.

### *Emotional Development*

Many parents will confess that a variety of emotions transform their (sometimes) cooperative, cheerful fifth-graders into (sometimes) moody, easily frustrated eighth-graders. The volunteers who work with young people in junior high will attest to their tendency to be sad one moment and giggly the next. The fluctuations in moods seem to be frequent, and the moods themselves often seem exaggerated, with youth who are happier than a good situation deserves and sadder than a bad one merits. If adults would eliminate about half of what they hear about this moodiness, they would have a good starting place for understanding emotional development in adolescence.

Emotional fluctuations in early adolescence may be influenced by the chemical changes that occur as new hormones are released into maturing bodies. Body chemistry influences mood and emotions throughout life, and there is no reason to assume it has no influence in adolescence. The assumption of many adults that early adolescents will always exhibit exaggerated emotions, however, may be as much the reason for the moodiness as hormonal changes. While moodiness can be very disruptive in a group or family, it is not the most important issue in adolescent emotional development.

*Identity.* A more important emotional agenda involves perception of the self. As the body rapidly matures and secondary sexual characteristics develop, the young person is confronted with an image of self that is very different from earlier images. Adolescents, according to Erik Erikson, spend considerable emotional energy dealing with identity, struggling to see if the way they see themselves is similar to the way they are seen by others.[3] The question of identity is not just "Who am I?" It is better understood in terms of "Do other people see me the way I see myself?" The struggle with identity in the context of relationships with others contributes to the youthful tendency to be peer-oriented.

The identity issue is further complicated in western society because of the number of choices adolescents have. The more choices one has to make, the more those choices are likely to create problems with identity. When a society tells someone, "You are this gender, this race, this social caste; therefore, you will do these things for the rest of your life," that person may have to deal with feelings of entrapment but not with problems of identity. On the other hand, when the society says, "You can work at whatever occupation you choose, marry whom you want, live wherever you want, hold to the values and style of life you choose—as long as your choices do not infringe on others' rights," adolescents must struggle with a myriad of options and may have trouble deciding who they are.

*Struggle.* Some youths do struggle with life, and the struggle can be very intense at times. Theologian Helmut Thielicke, in his analysis of the modern condition, refers to two kinds of despair,[4] and I have met more than a few young people with one of these two emotional reactions to life. The first is the desperate *wanting to be oneself.* Some young people are forever wanting to be themselves, to force friends or enemies to notice them, but no one does. They sulk in their rooms, alone and withdrawn. Others want to be themselves but are not sure who they are; they are one person one day and another person the next day, and troubled by both. The second is the desperate *wanting not to be oneself.* Some young people live with an unforgiving self-hatred. They do not like the bodies they have grown into, the parents they inherited, or their academic or athletic ability. They would give anything to have a differently shaped body, a different parent, or a different personality or to associate with another peer group.

These desperations can translate into affective problems such as depression. Most adolescents have occasional periods in which they feel down, but for some, depression becomes a persistent problem that requires special intervention.

*Altruism.* Adolescent years bring changes to other emotions. For example, the love for other people is different in adolescence from love felt during childhood years. Love grows more altruistic and less self-focused. There is still a sufficient dose of self-interest in a teenager's love of others, but he or she can also feel intense concern for the welfare and well-being of another person. A romantic relationship demonstrates the ability of youth to do things for the person loved: to give to, care for, and help.

*Intensity.* Young people tend to be emotionally intense persons. These emotions show up in the ways they laugh, cry, fall in love, feel despair, and enjoy life. Adults watch and frequently are inclined to ask them to "cool it" or "come down a notch." When adults push them toward more metered or mediated emotions, adolescents have a way of pushing back by feeling their emotions intensely, whether they express them that way or not.

### Behavioral Development

The significance and meaning of behavior, which changes during childhood years, changes again in adolescence. Young people behave in both testing and conforming ways.

Testing behavior doesn't start in adolescence. It goes back at least to early childhood and the how-bad-can-I-be-and-still-get-a-cookie test. Adolescents, however, are not behaving in ways that test only adult limits and standards. They are also testing their own limits and standards. They construct a part of their self-image around feats they have attempted or accomplished. Athletics, sexuality, socializing, and driving are frequent proving grounds for these behaviors. Testing can be ill-advised, even deadly. A parent confronting a son or daughter after some episode may say, "You never did anything this stupid before. What's wrong with you?" Testing behavior is intentional behavior, but not necessarily thoughtful behavior.

Conforming behavior is present, even exaggerated, with many teenagers. They do things they don't want to do or do things they know they shouldn't do; they don't like themselves when they do these things, but they do them anyway. Conforming behavior can be a ticket for admission to a peer group or the prerequisite for approval by others. And if the emotional rewards seem great enough, the young person behaves in conforming ways.

As human development continues, behavior moves from the impulsiveness of early childhood to the mediated meaningfulness of school-age years. The process continues in adolescence, but meanings are vested in the ability of behavior to provide indicators about parenthood, identity, and social relationships.

## Cognitive Development

It does not happen all at once, and it is not immediately obvious to anyone, but during the early to middle years of adolescence, young people begin to think differently from the way they did as children. The most striking change is that the individual becomes capable, for the first time in life, of conceptualizing abstract ideas.[5] For example, when children in elementary school discuss stories they have read, their discussions are frequently limited to retelling the story and identifying similar or different experiences in their own lives. In high school, however, adolescents are not limited to recounting the story. They can also analyze literature and discuss its many possible meanings. The ability to reflect on meaning is anchored to the adolescent's ability to think abstractly.

Adolescents seldom treat this developmental event in the same way they do their emerging sexual capacities. They do not rush out to explore it to the full extent that their conscience or a willing partner may allow! But the ability to think abstractly is developing and, with it, an entirely new way of viewing and interpreting the world.

Some developmentalists trace some of the emotional problems of this age group to the ability to think abstractly. Young people can use their ability to examine multiple possibilities. In addition to feeling lonely at times, they can also think about the phenomenon of loneliness and sometimes get depressed. They not only may feel rejected by their peers, they can also reflect on the nature of rejection, pursue its implications into the future, and become fearful and anxious.

The ability to think abstractly also explains why adolescents can be so idealistic. For the first time they can construct a reality based on principles and values. This idealism can influence religious experience in a variety of ways. It can fuel intense religious experience, as these young people seek to live out a faith that conforms to their idealized version. It can also induce a deep sense of failure when they realize they have not lived up to the ideals of their faith.

These developmental events identify some of the influences adolescents are experiencing from internal psychological promptings and reactions. Understanding them also requires an awareness of environmental influences. I would like you to consider a few of these environments: home and family, peers, and school, work, and church.

### Influential Environments

People live with so many stereotypes and assumptions about American adolescence that sometimes the truth is almost unbelievable. This is the case in discussions about the environments that influence youth. One of the more intriguing studies of American adolescents was conducted by researchers from the

University of Chicago's Committee on Human Development with a randomly selected sample of 2,700 high school students from Chicago area high schools.[6] The researchers gave the young people electronic beepers and asked them to record, among other things, what they were doing and where they were when the beeper was activated. From the resulting reports, the following data were compiled: 41 percent of the time the students were in their homes when they were beeped, 32 percent of the time they were in school, and 27 percent of the time they were in public environments such as with friends, in the car, at work, at the store, at church (0.8 percent of the time), or at recreational events.[7]

## Home and Family

These young people spent more time at home, on the average, than they did anywhere else. For half of the time they were at home, they were in their bedrooms, the yard, the garage, or the bathroom, so they were probably by themselves. The other half of their time at home, however, was spent in more public places like the kitchen, dining room, or living room—areas where they might have some interaction with other family members.

Home and family are environments of influence in the lives of youth. Family is less influential in adolescent years than it was in school-age childhood, but it is still influential. Part of the influence comes from parents and another part from siblings.

*Parents.* Many parents of adolescents falsely assume they no longer have power to influence them. Because they still remember the control they had when the children were young, they realize how much less they have now. Adolescents will be off in the car with their peers, they will be at school, or they will be at their friends' houses, and parents can no longer put them in the playpen or the car seat and order their whereabouts and activities. But parents can still exert influence. They can share the values that are important to them and explain why the life of faith is crucial to their way of seeing the world.

Parents can teach children of any age about what they consider important, and so order their own lives that adolescents can watch their parents live the values they espouse. The results are long-term. This kind of parenting doesn't eliminate bad moods, cantankerous moments, or fights in the car on the way to church. It does, however, give young people something to remember and, perhaps, to come back to on some future day.

When Search Institute researchers asked fifth- through ninth-graders to respond to the statement, "There is a lot of love in my family," 74 percent of these early adolescents in their sample of nearly 8,000 answered either "very true" or "quite true."[8] In the same study, these adolescents were given a series of situations and asked whom they would turn to for help. Even the responses of the ninth-graders indicated that they were more likely to turn to their parents than their peers when having trouble in school, wondering how to handle their feelings, or deciding what to do with their lives.[9]

*Siblings.* Another influential aspect of family life is the relationships of brothers and sisters. In a sense, interactions between brothers and sisters are the first place where human sin shows up and the last place from which it is redeemed. People who love every stranger on the street can still hate their brother or sister. Young people frequently feel their most intense forms of competition not with peers but with siblings and feel their greatest amount of rejection not from a peer group but from siblings and their friends. Not all sibling influence is negative, of course. Some teenagers find their best friends among brothers or sisters and have their best times when they are with them.

Siblings do exert influence. Older brothers and sisters frequently think they had it rougher than their younger siblings have it. Others feel they must assume the role of peacemaker because they get along with brothers and sisters who can't get along with each other. Still others, the youngest, feel competition with older siblings. Studies of the number of children in a family, birth order, and the kinds of roles families ascribe to different children in the family suggest that all these variables are potentially influential.

## Peers

Peer group affiliations, of course, provide an important influence for American youth. While the influence of the peer group over all areas of a young person's life is frequently exaggerated, it does hold considerable power over some areas. Peers are not all-powerful, but they do have some power.

The peer group functions in several ways. Perhaps the most significant function is to provide companions for recreation and leisure. In the Chicago study mentioned earlier, young people described the most pleasant part of their days as the time they were with friends and typically reported that time spent with friends involved more interactive activities than time spent with family.[10] For example, they most frequently reported that leisure time with family was spent watching television, but that leisure time with friends involved activities where they were joking with each other, talking to each other, the kinds of things involved in "hanging out."

The peer group can also provide a sense of status and identity for an adolescent. Different peer groups tend to have different social statuses in high schools, and inclusion in some peer groups elevates status while exclusion lowers it. The status a peer group provides may help some young people feel more positively about themselves, but the status effect of peer groups has more potential for negative than positive consequences. Adolescents excluded from a high-status peer group may have trouble feeling good about themselves, and those accepted into a high-status group may confuse their status as members of an envied group for a personal status bestowed on them as individuals. Some young adults who were a part of the most envied peer group in school and at the center of everything never are able to find themselves later in meaningful adult activity. When the group—and the status it gave—is gone, they are not quite sure what to do.

## School, Work, and Church

Most adolescents have the opportunity to participate in a wide world of involvements. School is the most central of these. An environment that also absorbs an increasing amount of time for older adolescents is the workplace. School and work are similar in the pressures they place on youth and the experiences they provide. Both environments tend to be performance-oriented, with periodic indications of whether work has been done well or poorly. Both tend to be environments where an abundance of peer influence exists in the midst of some adult supervision and expectation. Both environments provide opportunities for gratification and potential for failure.

Church is an environment of particular interest for this book. The influence of the community of faith seems to increase for some persons and decrease for others as they grow from childhood to adolescence. The youth volunteers in almost any congregation can identify some young people who are active in everything, involved and cooperative with anything the youth group at church does. Those same volunteers can also mention those who were active as children and early adolescents, whose families have been active in the church for years, but who scarcely participate in anything anymore. Adolescents, like adults, have no one reaction to church— either positive or negative. In an annual survey of 16,000 high school seniors in the mid-1980s, to the question "How important is religion in your life?" 52 percent of all black youth and 28 percent of all white youth responded with the most positive response possible, "very important." Of those who attended church once a week or more, 74 percent of black seniors and 56 percent of white seniors responded that religion was "very important" in their lives.[11] These data suggest that for the young people who are active at church, religion is a significant and important issue. The community of faith is an influential environment to those who participate regularly, and, while less influential for those who participate less frequently, it still has some shaping influence.

Adolescents differ from children in that they are more able to choose their environments. Parents are more willing to negotiate church attendance with older adolescents than they are with children. Some young people will withdraw from church activities and cannot be enticed back by any efforts that the congregation might extend to them. Others will come to church testing every person they meet. Adult leaders sometimes confuse this testing behavior, as well as signs of boredom or disinterest, as convincing indicators that these persons cannot be positively influenced at church. In the privacy of responding to a survey at school, however, many students affirm the importance of religion in their lives. Adult leaders at church do some of their best work with youth when they assume that church can be an influential environment.

## Youth and Faith

The developmental and environmental influences adolescents encounter do not determine their experience and expression of faith. They do, however, provide a context in which faith is experienced. For young people, as for others, faith involves an openness to God, a transforming relational participation with the people and purposes of God, and a process of meaning-making.

While these dimensions are received and expressed with considerable ease in childhood, adolescents sometimes struggle with them, even to the point of rejection. This is particularly true of individuals who have grown up in church; they ask themselves questions about what to affirm and how to make sense of the conflicting values that exist around them. Two images provide an accurate perspective on the faith many young people experience. The first is affirmation, and the second is synthesis.

*Affirmation.* One way to envision the religious experience of adolescence is as a time in which the maturing individual makes some personal affirmation or rejection of the tradition of faith that family and church have bequeathed. G. Temp Sparkman characterizes the decision this way: "No one involuntarily becomes a contributing part of the community of faith or a believer in Jesus Christ." The young person comes to a time in which "she must declare herself concerning Jesus Christ."[12] In spite of prior rituals of welcome or expressions of inclusion into the believing community, young people go through a process of either affirming or rejecting the sacred story they have heard and accepted as children.

Adolescents vary in the intensity and intentionality with which they struggle through this process of affirmation. For some, real affirmation comes quietly, peaceably, almost imperceptibly. For others, it comes only after battles, denials, and wrestling with a collection of people. Still others are more apathetic than rebellious, more aloof than embattled; faith remains something people at church have, which they may avail themselves of if time or circumstances should someday warrant. And for still others, there is an active, even volatile rejection of the faith they have been given by parents and church.

The process of affirmation is not something dealt with in a once-and-for-all fashion in adolescence. This may be the first time an individual feels a need to ask these questions and seek some inner resolution, but it will not be the last time. The seasons of adulthood will force the questions to the surface again, sometimes with the same intensity and sometimes with much greater force.

*Synthesis.* Another image that makes sense to me is that, as young people experience a broader range of involvements and feel the conflicts evident among those various aspects of life, they need to synthesize the discrepancies in one way or another. James Fowler suggests that one way to deal with the disparities is by clinging to a single position and rejecting others. Another way is to reflect the prevailing position of the environment. Young people who choose the first approach may accept the values and influence of the church environment to the exclusion of most other environments or, in a similar manner, may reject church altogether and affirm the values maintained in some other environment. Those who resolve the disparity by the second approach sometimes live life one way with their friends and another way when at church; occasionally, they question whether or not something is terribly wrong with them because they act so differently in different settings.[13]

Sparkman's and Fowler's characterizations of typical faith experience in adolescence describe two different, fundamentally important aspects of faith. Affirmation and commitment require considerable cognitive effort, but their power to shape life is rooted in affect, in emotion. They deal with an openness to God and a willingness to participate in the purposes of God. Synthesizing meaning and interpreting disparity evoke emotions which, at their roots, emerge from cognitive analysis. It has more to do with the meaning-making element of faith experience.

The faith of youth is shaped and influenced by participation in the community of faith and by that community's expressions of ministry.

## Ministry with Youth

Congregations have frequently worried about youth and the youth ministry the church is providing more than they have worried about other age groups and the ministry directed toward them. There may be good reason for this. Some important issues are at stake. Adolescents may be at a *kairos* time in their emerging faith. They will make decisions that can be more far-reaching than any they made as children. Those who nurture the faith of youth should be sensitive to the significance of this period of life. Young people are intellectually and emotionally capable of faith expressions and experiences that were not possible during childhood. A ministry of nurture needs to provide a variety of resources to help identify, struggle with, and affirm the Christian story that has been shared with them. I would like to introduce areas and approaches to ministry that reflect the model of ministry presented in chapter 6.

*Worship.* Adolescents can be nurtured through the worship life of the community of faith. For the first time, they have all the cognitive resources necessary to understand and evaluate what is being said and done. They are also emotionally sensitive to those aspects of corporate worship that invite people to affirm their faith and experience the presence of God. Young people benefit from worship that takes them seriously. They will be more likely to listen to the sermon if the preacher, without condescending, uses illustrations that reflect his or her awareness of the world in which they live and if the preaching occasionally addresses the problems they experience. Young people are very aware of persons. To the extent the preacher takes them seriously and is willing to engage them outside of worship and church settings, the preacher's sermons will be taken more seriously.

Adolescents are frequently energized in worship when it conveys enduring truth and images in engaging and creative ways. They attend worship with remarkably little allegiance to practices that are done primarily because they have always been done. By their insistence on "what does this mean?" they provide adults with the opportunity to affirm the meanings of their modes and methods of worship. Young people will learn about worship as they have opportunity to participate in worship leadership and as their needs are addressed, as consciously and conspicuously as the needs of persons of other ages are addressed.

*Spiritual life.* Adolescents are not only capable of embracing the ways of prayer and spiritual discipline that have marked the believing community, they are more inclined to experiment with them and attempt them than are many adults. This is a good time in life for individuals to be invited on retreat, to evaluate what it means to be the people of God, and to be exposed to the variety of spiritual disciplines.

Some of you reading these paragraphs are probably asking yourselves if I know any young people like the ones you have in your churches. You think I'm portraying an overly optimistic view of youth. The adolescents you know won't participate in anything, won't listen in worship, and wouldn't say a prayer or read a scripture passage under any circumstances! There are individuals like this in most churches—just as there are adults who want nothing more from congregational involvement than their name on the church roll. Not all young people can be reached, not all will respond, not all will find the issues of faith anywhere on their personal agenda. Ministry with youth requires a continuing invitation to these young people, and it demands that they be known one at a time. What may be true for the youth group may *not* be true for each adolescent in that group.

The spiritual life involves life together, but it also invites people into solitary places where they may experience communion with God. Even in the midst of a lethargic youth group, there are frequently those who are seekers after faith. These individuals especially need the encouragement and care of others.

Adolescents are capable of spiritual genius. Thérèse of Lisieux was fifteen when she entered the Carmelite order. She died at twenty-seven, leaving a legacy of spiritual sensitivity that was recognized by her canonization in 1925. Mary, when she gave birth to Jesus, and David, when he seized faith and faced Goliath, were both adolescents by contemporary American standards. Many American church youth may be more interested in MTV than exploring the parameters of classical Christian spirituality. But there are young people in the churches who possess a passion for God, who have an emotionality that is venturesome, who have a spiritual hunger that lingers after the mass is said or the worship service is over.

*Moral life.* There is a chapter to write on this point. Youth struggle with a variety of moral choices, many with life-changing consequences. Parents—and other adults who care—gather in church basements and look for ways to protect these young people from the negative consequences of bad moral choices and for methods of instruction that will guarantee they make right decisions.

Parents and church youth workers must remind themselves that all people have been created as free moral agents. No way of parenting or ministering with youth will guarantee that young people will learn the right and always do it. Some learn about the right and choose to do the wrong. Like the rest of the human family, they choose to sin. Churches should do everything they can to nurture the moral life of youth, but they can do nothing that will guarantee the outcome of their efforts.

Young people can learn moral categories, and the things they learn at church can make a difference in how they live their lives. They need to encounter both personal moral issues and social moral concerns. Personal moral issues include concerns such as substance abuse and sexuality, and social moral concerns relate to issues such as peace and justice. Parents tend to be more readily concerned about personal morality, but the community of faith can present both moral dimensions.

Using alcohol or drugs for entertainment, to alter moods, or to deal with stress and anxiety is not something only adolescents do. It is an adult pattern of behavior too. While there is no guaranteed successful program to prevent substance abuse at any age, there is an emerging profile of those who are least likely to be abusers. Young people who are more involved in people-helping activities, express more confidence that the future holds promise, are more affirming of religion, have better friendship-making and communication skills, are involved in adult-supervised programs and activities, attend schools with firm policies about drug use that are strictly enforced, and have parents who set rules about drug use and monitor compliance are less likely to become substance abusers than are those for whom these characteristics are not descriptive.[14] Many of these perspectives can be facilitated through attitudes and activities that are part of the congregational youth ministry program. Congregations can do nothing to isolate youth either from society and its prevailing attitudes or from peers and the pressure they may exert, but they can encourage some of the attitudes and provide some of the activities that will help.

The moral issues associated with teenage sexuality are also complex. Some data clearly suggest that young people who are active in church or who consider religion important are less likely to be sexually active than those who are not active in church or do not consider religion as important. Young people who believe it is morally wrong to have sexual intercourse outside of marriage are more likely to abstain from genital sexual activity than those who do not think it wrong.[15] Isn't that amazing: Beliefs that youth hold about what is right and what is wrong can actually influence behavior!

While parents and youth leaders are less readily energized about social moral issues, they comprise an important aspect of the Christian gospel. Teenagers tend, in this area as well, to follow society's lead. As Americans in general have grown less concerned during the last fifteen years over such social moral issues as peace, justice, racial prejudice, human rights, and the poor and oppressed, successive generations of youth have tended to register less concern over these issues.[16] The community of faith bears a responsibility to witness to the whole gospel and speak to issues of social as well as personal moral significance. On the one hand, the self-preoccupation of many young people inhibits them from automatically attending to issues such as social justice. On the other hand, the idealism that comes naturally to many teenagers can turn their concern toward these issues, when they are appropriately nurtured and prompted.

*Pastoral life.* One of the memories I have of the young people I worked with at the church mentioned at the beginning of this chapter is our Sunday afternoon visits to a residential facility for mentally retarded persons. It was a facility built for custodial care, underfunded and understaffed. The youth group from our church volunteered to spend time with severely retarded children. They played with the children and provided personal care. The children were helped, but the volunteers were changed. They learned about giving to people who couldn't even know they were receiving. They learned about care and, in the process, they learned about the gospel of God.

Teenagers can be involved in the life of care and service to others. They are good at it. Working on a mission team, helping indigent persons, working with aged persons in the church, tutoring young children, and helping with summer recreation programs can all be formative influences for them. Sometimes in the concrete experience of activities they can discover themselves, what they believe, and what they should value more readily than they can in Sunday night discussion groups.

*Education.* The formal educational ministry with youth should focus on one primary agenda. With their emerging ability to think in formal operational ways, adolescents need to rethink their faith. Now that they have the developing ability to think in abstractions, they can begin for the first time to explore the significance of the symbols and rituals they have experienced in church. They now have the capacity to consider the meanings of the stories they have learned. They need the kind of educational experiences that do more than rehash the events and details of the biblical story. They need to be invited to consider its meaning. Young people will construct a theology. It may be untutored and unreflective, but most of them will develop answers for classic religious questions. A nurturing community can help them construct a theology that is doctrinally literate and personally reflective.

These goals are not met by inviting teenagers to sit down for an intensive time period and think through every doctrine the church holds dear. They learn over the years, by the influence of models who patiently and persistently push them in the direction of reflection and evaluation.

*Community.* Adolescents are sensitive to and influenced by the people who work with them. They will learn more from people in church than from the literature they will be asked to read there. Ministry with youth needs vigilantly to introduce young people to volunteers and ministers who will take them seriously, who can invite them to claim the adultlike person that is emerging in them, who will help them envision a gospel dream and feel forgiveness when they fail, and who are people of faith. Many churches have done youth a disservice by recruiting volunteers who were the most athletic or energetic or youngest adults in the congregation. These may be characteristics of some people who are good with teenagers, but they are not qualifications. Ministry with youth should be vested in people who are caring, who are real, who are open to the teenagers and their high-energy world, and who have an authentic faith they can make available.

In the same service that Andrea read her poem and made her remarks, our Minister of Youth directed the congregation's attention to youth with these words:

How do we develop capable young people? First, we must grow children up in love and trust, letting them know they are loved by a kind God who accepts and affirms them; then, as they grow older, we begin giving them sequences of freedom, thereby proclaiming that we endorse whom God has ordained to become the new generation. We give them the freedom to choose Christ. We give them the freedom to sit in the balcony. Along the way, we also give them responsibility. . . . Finally, we give capable roles where the youth gain for themselves the trust and love that responsibility fosters.[17]

I was struck by the summary truth in his brief introduction. Young people who were blessed as preschoolers and included as elementary children are now given freedom to say "yes" and responsible acts of service to carry out.

# 8

# Paying Attention to Adults

*What are some of your fears?*

*Honestly, the only thing that really comes to me that I would be fearful of . . . is [for] my children. You know, with the kind of world we live in, that . . . one of our children would be drawn in the wrong direction.*

—A woman in her early thirties

*What do you think it means to be a believing person?*

*My profession is the advertising business, and so to me to be a believing person means I am a believer. In other words, I don't say one thing and do another; my faith is acted out in my life. My words aren't going one way and my life another. The funny thing about my advertising is that advertising is strong stuff, but it does not overcome the truth. What I am speaks louder than what I say.*

—A man in his early fifties

*What kinds of things do you fear?*

*I like life, but I realize it is a terrific challenge. And I don't want to do anything that would deny the life I try to teach. . . . You have so many people around you that can be affected by you. I don't want anybody to stumble over me.*

—A woman in her late sixties

A baby's first time at church attracts more attention than does attendance on most subsequent Sundays. A person's last time at church, in a coffin for a funeral, attracts more praise and high regard than most of the other times the individual was there. Beginnings create interest, evoke hope, and engender celebrations. Endings invite memory, evoke grief, and, in the best of times, engender thanksgiving. Middles are very different. They are more muddling and maudlin. If anything, they tend to invite presumption and disregard. Adulthood is the long-term middle of life. Adulthood does have its developmental flow, but it is more subtle, less spectacular, less observable, and far more highly individualized than the developmental movement in earlier times of life.

Beginnings may be more flashy, and endings may evoke more sentiment, but paying attention to people demands considerable attention to the long haul of the middle of life. The people whose comments opened this chapter reflect the longings of adulthood: the parental longing for children to be preserved in the face of threat; the religious longing to be congruent in both the affirmations and actions of one's faith; the personal longing to stand by the meanings one has made in life. These life concerns show up in church because most of the people there are adults.

Intentional congregations and parishes will make a place for children and youth, but even the most casual and unreflective congregations will provide adult-oriented activities and worship events. In some ways, adulthood is the "default" era of life. Children and youth require special space and special programming. But when congregations are not thinking "special," they are typically thinking "adult." The result is not always as beneficial for the grown-ups as one might first assume. Typical patterns of thinking easily become presumptuous patterns of thinking, full of assumptions that may be inaccurate and misleading.

In this chapter, I want to characterize adult development with particular emphasis on the influential contexts and factors in adult life. Then the focus shifts to the adult experience of faith, with its theological reflection and need for nurture by the community of faith.

## A Perspective on Development in Adulthood

What happens in adulthood that can rightly be characterized as human development? In chapter 4, I identified two basic questions a developmental theory must address: ( 1 ) What most influences human development? and ( 2 ) What happens in the developmental process? The second question is the one before us now, and I want to respond to it in terms of the possibilities mentioned in the earlier chapter. The developmental process can be perceived as a series of sequential stages, each with certain issues and agenda, or it can be seen as an ongoing process of learning.

A developmental stage perspective of adulthood maintains that different internal psychological influences are introduced at different points in life that interact with external events and result in an identifiable developmental process. For example, in Erikson's theory of adulthood, the young adult must deal with a psychological agenda concerning intimacy and isolation in relationships; middle-aged adults deal with the tension between generativity and stagnation; older adults are confronted with the tension between the integrity that comes from affirming what one's life has been and the despair that comes from the failures, pain, and apparent meaninglessness of life.[1] Adult stage theory has become very influential, particularly in the work of Erik Erikson, Daniel Levinson, and George Vaillant.[2]

A learning perspective construes adult development as an extended process of learning. Life presents events and circumstances, and people learn from them. The resulting learning history influences how adults see the world, themselves, their future, and their past. Different life experiences and different reactions to those events mean that adult development is predictable only in the sense that people learn, and that learning influences their lives.[3]

I tend to see the developmental process in adulthood in more singular terms than development in earlier periods of life. Let me explain. With children and youth, I think cognitive development proceeds the way Jean Piaget has described it and, as such, is a stage-related phenomenon—with all the technical implications of a stage theory. Because of the central influence of cognitive ability on several other areas of life, including emotionality and behavior, much of the developmental process is best understood in terms of stages. However, stage development is not the only process at work. Children and adolescents also learn, and their learning explains many other developmental events. As individuals move into adulthood, the developmental impetus stems more from learning experiences than internal stage sequence. Two influential processes in childhood and adolescence give way to one process that continues throughout adulthood.

This perspective reflects a position on the other basic question a developmental theory addresses: What most influences development? Is it more influenced by internal psychological events or by external environmental events? While both influences are present, the increased role of learning in adulthood means that the environmental and contextual influences take on greater importance than the internal forces do.

Adults, all through their lives, have been influenced by internal psychological factors. Fears and anxieties from earlier life periods will influence present attitudes and behavior. The position I am proposing is not that an adult's experience of life events is the determinative influence on all psychological characteristics. Rather, it is that life events, and the individual's reactions to them and reflections on them, create the context for the learning that is the most crucial element in adult development.

If adult development is more related to learning than to internal psychological scripting, it is far less predictable than other periods of development. Experiences vary and adult reactions to them also vary. The result is that adults put life together in a variety of ways, and there is no one way of forecasting how a particular individual will develop. Individual developmental paths are anchored to events and to individual reactions to those events. The common themes in adult development are caused at least as much by the similar contexts adults encounter as by any internal psychological mapping.

Adult development, in the perspective of this chapter, is defined as the process of learning, reacting, and reflecting on life as the adult encounters tasks, roles, and events.

## Influential Contexts and Factors in Adult Life

If adults develop through their encounters of and reactions to life events, then the contexts they most commonly experience have profound importance. The contexts of greatest influence, in my opinion, date back to primordial origins, which in the language of the Bible was a garden.

The story of the human family's founding has a number of plots, but none are more noticeable than these three: the work that was to be done in the midst of the garden, the relationships that were a part of life in the garden, and the nature of the human creation of male and female. It is intriguing that the Bible's creation narrative tells not of the birth of babies reared by God but of the creation of adults who come into an environment readied for work, companionship, and reproduction.

### Gaining and Giving: Vocation and Work

Work was there, in the garden, before sin. According to the narrative of Genesis 2, "The LORD God took the man and put him in the garden of Eden to till it and keep it" (v. 15). Work, along with the rest of creation, was made good. As the story unfolds, sin came, and with the fall, work was cursed with drudgery. The tilling became toiling. In the beginning, work was good; in the fall, it became layered with evil. Work is best seen as a theological reality, not just a sociological or economic fact of life. The theological significance of work influences how we look at it and what we do with it. It also means that both sin and redemption have a way of manifesting themselves in the work that adults do.

At one level, work is a very practical part of adulthood. Most adults need to work their way through life. We make things, provide services, keep houses, raise children, till the soil, and teach others what we know. Work sometimes provides income, and sometimes it meets the needs of children and families. For many, work also provides the means by which they hope to make things better for their families, for themselves, or for their community.

At another level, work appears to mean more for adults than

merely accumulating income or making a contribution. Work provides a context in which adults can have some psychological needs met, according to Erikson. Work also has a way of attracting the more shadowy, less healthy side of people. Instead of work's being the basis for income or contribution, it becomes a desperate attempt to prove something. Instead of its being used as a means, it is pursued as a saving end, as if it were something that could heal wounds and mend brokenness. James Dittes identifies several ways in which work degenerates into a status it cannot live up to.[4] When adults value work inappropriately, they can push themselves into depression or burnout; they can make an idol of work and become addicted to it.

Work can also shift from providing income needed for survival to the accumulation of power, either through position or wealth. Power and wealth, in the wisdom of the scripture, have a peculiar tendency to become idols.[5] When this happens, people use their religious sentiment to pursue a security that is surely false and obtain an invulnerability that is fragile and weak.

Work has the potential of being productive, rewarding, even fulfilling for adults. When work is in its place and does its job, it contributes to adults' well-being and encourages developmental lines to fall in pleasant places. When work is distorted and asked to provide more than it can, adult development stumbles onto a road with deep ruts and bruising potholes. Work can be a way of gaining enough to live, a way of giving oneself for the benefit of others, and a way of making a contribution to some future good. It can also become a relentless taskmaster that requires more and more and gives less and less.

Anyone's work can have either effect, but the more work provides the opportunity for making meaningful contributions, or accumulating significant wealth, the more work itself can become the boss. A day laborer on a construction crew may not assume his work will make him famous or wealthy and may never become as addicted to it as has the owner of the construction company, who has built a frail sideline into a successful business. A person who works at a fast food restaurant and sees very little social contribution to the task may be less tempted to overinvest in work than a person working in ministry, where all tasks can be readily envisioned as making some significant contribution to others. There is virtually no job that cannot provide meaning and fulfillment for some adults, and virtually none that cannot attract false expectations, overinvestment, and debilitating frustration.

Work, like the other realities that were in the garden, is neither sinful nor virtuous. It is work. But it becomes a complex context in which adults work out parts of their development, sometimes in saintly ways and sometimes in more sinful ways as well.

### Leaving and Cleaving: Relationships

A second significant characteristic of life in the garden was that humans were created for relationship. The stories vary in their details about relationship, but relationship is so central to the human creation that the biblical texts explain the origin of relationships more than once. Adam and Eve were together in the garden, given the gift of relationship with each other and with the God who had made them. When sin came, the relationship between the man and the woman was fractured, as well as the relationship they both had with the Creator. Like work, relationship was a good part of creation that was broken in the fall. Relationships, like work, also become an aspect of adult life where the effects of both sin and redemption are on display.

Individuals struggle with relationships for much of their lives, but in adulthood the intensity of relationships is heightened and their expanse is broadened. Middle-aged adults, for example, are frequently dealing simultaneously with relationships with their children, with other adults their own age, and with aging parents. A woman is mother, friend, wife, and daughter. A man is father, friend, husband, and son. Adults sometimes discover very different parts of themselves in these different relationships, and it is not uncommon for these parts to conflict with each other.

Most American adults marry, most have other adult friends,

most have children, and all have had parents. I would like to reflect briefly on these kinds of relationships.

*Marriage and sexual relationships.* The relationships that end up in marriage—and which end marriages—are complex even at their most simple level. These relationships evoke some of the most intense dreams and altruistic hopes human beings can conceive. They also provide the setting where intimate rage is expressed and anger—which is successfully secluded from life's other interactions—is vented. Marriage provides the context where an adult's vulnerability is never too far out of the picture, and where a sense of self is never able to maintain the facade that more casual company permits. Intimacy and vulnerability, self-disclosure and self-doubt are themes that frequently find their way through marriage relationships. They are surprisingly mingled with celebration, warmth, a sense of well-being, and love.

The loss of marriage by death or divorce is as painful and threatening an experience as many adults will ever experience. Even deaths that come gently in due time and divorces that confirm a mutual dissolution of love prove more devastating in their reality than they were in their anticipation. A romantic relationship—the real I-love-you-and-you-love-me kind—engages adults at such fundamental levels of their person that ending the relationship bares the threat of ending part of the self as well.

*Children.* The parent-child relationship is different from the adult romantic relationship, but it captures adults at just as deep a level. I talked to two parents in our church the other day. If I wanted to illustrate how to raise children with integrity, love, commitment, and skill, I would simply describe them. They are both warmhearted and clearheaded in their parenting. I was talking to them because their high school son had recently been admitted to the hospital for drug and chemical dependency treatment. They hurt at a part of their being that is untouched by any other pain. The threat of a child's devastating dependency is a pain that is not easily comforted and does not go away quickly. When parents lose children to death, the words of Jeremiah quoted in Matthew ring true: "Rachel weeping for her children; she refused to be consoled" (Matt. 2:18). It is not just the refusal to be consoled, it is the inability to be comforted.

The effort required by parenting bonds parents to children in ways the children may never be bonded to their parents. The vulnerability an infant brings to the world never quite leaves a parent's perspective of that child. Even grown, parents see the fragility of life in their children in ways they cannot see in their own lives. Adults who take the parental task seriously are captured by this spectacle of vulnerability and haunted by their increasing inability to protect their children from harm. Good parenting begins by keeping little children close; holding and protecting are good for both their physical and psychological well-being. But good parenting continues by learning how to let go and help children find their way in the world. It is an awkward task: doing the opposite of one's impulses in order to implement the care they represent.

In the context of this relationship, with its emotions, physical fatigue, worry, and exhilaration, adults learn a great deal about themselves and about life, and they change—they *develop*. Perspectives are renovated and meaning is reconstituted.

*Adults relating to parents.* Another relational environment that changes during the course of adulthood is the interaction between adult children and their parents. Some adult children still cling to parents for financial support, or child care, or help in crises. Other children feel an intense need to function independently from parents, almost to the point of rejecting normative expressions of parental love and help. Still others find their way into comfortable relationships of mutual respect, care, and support.

Most younger adults find ways to relate to parents, and most parents discover the ins and outs of being parents to adult children. In the process, both parents and children are changed, and a period of stable expectations and interactions follows for many years. Then new agendas emerge. Parents age their way into new life needs and sometimes require different kinds of attention from their children. The children become the care-givers. The parent who has constructed an entire adulthood around care-giving, self-sufficiency, and productivity is sometimes forced to become the care-receiver and deal with the trauma of being less self-sufficient and less productive.

Adult children may eventually go to the funeral home one day and stand before a casket that holds a parent. And whether the child is forty and the parent sixty-five or the child is sixty and the parent is eighty-five, the experience has a way of evoking intense emotions. In that moment the grown-up children become the senior adults in their family. The last childlike assumption that "my parent knows things that can help me" must now be abandoned. Not infrequently, the unresolved tensions that stalked their way through a lifetime now lie like open wounds. A parent unable to bless a child in life will not be able to bless in death, and that child will walk away from the funeral with two griefs: that the parent is gone and that, to the end, the blessing the child so longed to receive never came. A child unable to appreciate a parent's heroic efforts in life finally realizes them in death and walks away from the graveside with one grief that will heal—that a parent has died—and another grief that may haunt the individual for years—that of never expressing sufficient appreciation or care.

*Friendship.* Adults experience still another kind of relationship in their friendships. These relationships do not have much similarity to the friendships of childhood or adolescence. Adult friendships can provide mutual care and support and the sense of empowerment that comes from being accepted and understood, in addition to ongoing companionship in life.

Adults who marry and have children may experience their friendships differently from the way single adults do. While the demands of marriage and parenting make friendships very important, family responsibilities frequently drain away energy that could be invested in them. Single adults are often able to give more energy, with the result that their friendships provide greater support and intimacy. Friends can become a family, just as family members can become friends.

A host of other reactions typically occur in adult relationships. I have listed some familiar ones only for the purposes of

illustration. These descriptions may seem presumptuous or out
of touch. Not everyone marries, not everyone has children,
not everyone has parents whom they ever knew, and some
people live through adulthood with few, if any, friends. I do
not mean to imply that adults who are single, or who are
childless, or who have never known a parent are stunted in
adult development. On the contrary, they will develop
through adulthood by the experiences and influences that provide the grist for their lives, to which they react, and on which
they reflect.

There are as many ways of being influenced in adult development as there are individual adults who experience unique
life events. I have mentioned relationships in the way that I
have, and to the extent that I have, because relationships,
whatever their form, are profoundly powerful forces. They
engage adults in their emotions and behaviors, in the way they
experience the joy and pain of life, and provide the context for
much of life's reflection.

### Gender

Back in the garden, after time began, human beings were
made male and female. And from the beginning the narrative
talks about this difference in terms of gender roles as well as
differences in anatomy. It is the roles and the implication of
roles that energize gender as a developmental influence.

During much of young childhood, a child is unaware of
gender. For example, Jenny asked me one day when she was
three years old if she would grow up to be a man or a woman.
She was becoming aware of gender, but her awareness was not
yet clear. During school-age years, many children spend considerable time with friends of the same gender. They become
aware that they are boy or girl, and their initial reaction, in this
society, is to accept similar-sex persons and reject opposite-sex
persons. Then, by adolescence, they become more interested
in opposite-sex persons and find them embracingly different.
In adulthood, gender creates questions like: What does it mean
to be man or woman? What choices do I have for the way in

which I will lead my life? Why do I choose what I choose? What do I do with the gender I am and the expectations people place on me because of it?

*Gender and development.* These questions represent the reason I am proposing gender as an influence on adult development. In childhood and adolescence, individuals learn that they have gender, are socialized to gender roles, and discover how they can relate to others in sexual ways. Adults must determine how much of the gender role that was handed to them will remain acceptable. They are confronted by the abstract gender expectations society places on them and the concrete assumptions reflected in everyday interactions. In a society that values free choice, on the one hand, and maintains gender role expectations, on the other, this issue creates the context for developmental tension. Unlike work and relationships that are influential throughout adulthood, gender is a more significant context in the first half of adulthood than the last.

A part of the response a person makes to gender is likely to be related to an assumption or conviction about the origins of gender differences. There are psychologists who argue that women differ from men in their psychological disposition and way of experiencing the world because of genetic endowment.[6] Other psychologists argue that the differences in psychological characteristics are more a function of a society's socializing influences than genes.[7] Regardless of the origins of the differences, men and women do differ in more than their anatomy. I would like you to consider a few images as a way of exploring these differences.

*Man as chairman of the board and as father of the groom.* Have you ever noticed what the father of the groom does at the wedding? In my ministry, the father of the groom is about as close to nonbeing as an individual can become. Sometimes he may be a best man or groomsman, but short of that the wedding would proceed just fine if the father of the groom weren't even present! The father of the bride may escort the bride to the altar, the mother of the groom will be ceremonially seated at the proper time by the proper usher. But the father of the groom remains inconspicuously sidelined during this significant celebration of his son's marriage. Like the flowers, he is supposed to look nice and stay in place. I'm exaggerating, of course, but it is not gross exaggeration.

Now put that father in the corporate boardroom, officers of the company on either side, senior executives at the other end of the table. He sits at the table in the chairman's chair. His is no awkward presence in this room, no incidental inclusion, no sideline participation.

These two scenes reflect two areas of high drama. A wedding is a celebration of adult relationship. It is the only formal celebration in this culture where a relationship between two adults is solemnized. A corporation boardroom is a place where the most successful workers do their jobs. The chairman is the one whose job it is to provide wise guidance. He is the quintessential successful American worker.

American males, for whatever the reasons, are more intimately identified with work than with relationship. A number of studies and observations about male development reflect this tendency.[8] Men appear to find their identity in work and productivity more readily than they find it in relationships. They are inclined to abandon relationships if those relationships become too intrusive on work. Some of their most intense failures are work-related. Men, whether because of their genes or the way in which they have been raised in this society, tend to encounter more developmental influences from their success and failure with work than their success and failure in relationships.

*Woman as mother of the bride and as member of the office team.* Now return to the wedding scene and consider one additional image. This time, the focus is on the mother of the bride. She is the last to be seated before the ceremony and the first to be ushered from the sanctuary at its conclusion. It is the bride's day, but it is also a day for the mother of the bride.

It is different at the office. While the real picture is slowly changing, the caricature remains. At the office, the woman's desk is in the greeting area, in front of the door to the boss's office. When the important client arrives and the big decisions are to be made, the woman greets and hosts, but she returns to her desk while the decisions are made. She may be more capable than the boss, but she sits outside the office, to assist the boss and sometimes cover for him.

In the celebration of relationship, woman is present and noticeable, down front in plain view. In the consummation of the big deal, the boss's door is frequently shut while she sits at the desk out front. Being down front at church for a wedding is overwhelmingly different from being out front in the office when the executive decision is made.

Again, the pictures are exaggerated. Not all women reflect this distinction anymore than all men fit the previous one. There is some research, however, and some informed opinion from psychological studies of women by women, that women are more likely to focus their identity, and to interpret their successes and failures as adults, in terms of relationships more than in terms of productivity in a job. Career women, for example, tend to worry more about the effects of their careers on children or spouses than do career men. Some women are willing to leave careers to pursue relationship goals more readily than men are. Some observers—Carol Gilligan is one—construe relationship as the premier issue in the development of women.[9]

Some men build their adult lives around relationship and pay little attention to their work. Some women fashion their adult lives around work and career and show little need for relationships beyond the professional associations their careers require. Many men and women work very hard at both career and relationships and spend considerable energy in keeping these two influences equally at heart. Adults develop one person at a time, and development in adulthood is the most highly stylized of any time in life. But gender is a part of the developmental influence for many. It can pit desires, roles, social expectations, and personal longings against one another. It influences the ways adults put their lives together and evaluate what they have done.

## Developmental Contexts

Many other contexts of influence are possible, and the impact of each varies with individual adults. I have presented these three because they are influential in so many adult lives, because they influence adults in as many ways as they do, and because they reflect the ancient insights of the biblical tradition. Adult development, for me, is the process of learning, reacting, and reflecting on life as the adult encounters tasks, roles, and events that emerge from the contexts in which adults live.

## Adults and the Experience of Faith

Adults developing through their encounters with relationships, work, and gender bring reflections from those encounters to their faith. Adult faith experience is characterized in several ways. I would like, first, to summarize briefly some of those characterizations and, second, to suggest several theological themes that emerge in adult faith experience.

### Characterizations of Adult Faith

I have referred to the work of James Fowler frequently throughout these chapters. While questions can be raised about the process of faith development as he proposes it, and about the way in which he defines faith, the descriptions he has offered of different stages of faith are astute, empirically informed, and helpful. If the descriptions are not of "stages" of faith, they certainly reflect different "kinds" of faith experience that people possess and profess. In Fowler's theory, adults may be at any of several different stages of faith, but most likely at one of two.

*Synthetic.* The synthetic-conventional stage was introduced in chapter 7, because it frequently first appears during adolescence. It continues, for many people, through much of adulthood. The diverse experiences of life, with their often competing positions, require the individual to attempt some form of synthesis. One way to synthesize is to choose one environment over all others and accept its affirmations of meaning and value. For many adults, church functions as such an environment. They affirm their particular community of faith, attempt to abide by its teaching, and employ its way of seeing the world over other possibilities.. They make good church members, of course, because meaning is exclusively vested in the church. They accept the doctrines expressed by the faith community as their own. However, because they have accepted these doctrines more than deliberated on them, these adults may be more inclined to defend than to discuss them. They may have problems because their vision stops short, and they may reject an alternative claim to truth before investigating it. They may be people of more religious conviction than insight.

Other adults with this same kind of faith experience synthesize the competing claims of truth by conforming to accepted standards and values of each of the environments in which their lives are lived. An adult with this style of faith can be an usher on Sunday morning and visibly identify with the values and convictions of the faith community—and, at work on Tuesday, conform to legal but unethical business practices because they are accepted norms of practice in his or her profession. When asked about the apparent contradiction in behavior from Sunday to Tuesday, this person may say something like "Church is church and business is business; that's just the way it is in the real world." Synthetic-conventional faith calls a truce between discrepant values and forces of meaning. It does little, however, to alleviate the inherent hostilities among them.

*Individuative.* The other stage of faith that adults at church typically reflect is one in which the individual is coming to terms both with the variety of values that life presents and with the need to arrive at some defensible and coherent conclusion about them. This kind of faith is, in Fowler's words, more individuative and more reflective. It sees competing claims to truth for what they are; it sees the polarities of human existence; it senses the adult responsibility to take a position that can be regarded as one's own. The faith of the community is no longer enough. The values of different environments can no longer be obliged just because one participates in each of those environments. Faith must be something the individual can claim and something the individual can defend. Because the individual finally has come to a personally owned position, its defense is sometimes more intense than circumstances warrant. Like the "no" of the young child who has finally found an identity and asserts it by refusing to do as the parent asks, this adult has found a personal faith and holds to it rigidly.[10]

A few other adults are at other stages. In Fowler's understanding of faith, only adults can experience the last three of six stages of faith.

*Creative trustees.* Another model that characterizes the differing contours of faith has been proposed by G. Temp Sparkman and referred to in earlier discussions. Sparkman's view of adult faith includes the central affirmation that, as individuals mature in their experience of faith, they become aware not only that they are redeemed children of God but also that they are trustees for God in the completion of creation.[11] As trustees, they live out a humility that emerges from the unexplainable and immeasurable mystery of God and live into their mission of active involvement in the world on behalf of God. Growth comes as adults learn, and considerable learning occurs as individuals reflect theologically on the experiences and events of life.

*Faith and learning.* I have been suggesting that learning plays an increasingly important role in the developmental lives of adults. Gabriel Moran's engaging study of development, education, and religion identifies two forms of learning that can have considerable impact during adulthood.[12] The first of these is job/work. Adults who are people of faith can learn to interpret the work they do in the context of the faith they hold. They can also learn that the job they do is not the only work to be done; they also have a religious vocation: to do the work of the people of God—the tasks of creative trusteeship, in Sparkman's words. The second of these is leisure/wisdom.

There is a learning that can only occur when the amount of experience has reached a sort of critical mass and when significant time for reflection is available. In this society, these conditions frequently do not exist until retirement. The work that people of faith do after retirement from their jobs involves the seasoned exercise of contemplation. The possibility of true wisdom emerges from this work.

The influences these kinds of learning bring to adult faith constitute a process of journeying and centering.[13] People who journey take the opportunity to take a second look at their faith, to reevaluate what they have claimed, and to reclaim what they come to value. They are inquirers, and eventually their journey will lead back to the center of being in God.

*Paying attention to adult faith.* Adulthood incorporates so much time, so many experiences, and so much individual reflection that the hue and texture of faith can be woven into many different designs and fabrics. The characterizations made by Fowler, Sparkman, and Moran are both insightful and helpful. These three people are cartographers; they have mapped the territory of adult faith experience. Their descriptions of faith are appropriately used as a way of paying attention to the people at church. That phrase, no doubt growing old by now, nevertheless continues to be an important one. Understanding different faith expressions helps identify the issues and tensions with which adults deal. And understanding those issues provides insight for the task of understanding who adults are.

### Adulthood and Theological Reflection

The process by which adults encounter life events and reflect on them inevitably raises theological themes. When life provides the agenda for theology, theology ceases to be mere formal propositional thought and becomes the individual's attempt to interpret the rhythms of life in the presence of God. The theology a person constructs will carve a far deeper pattern into that individual's faith than will propositions received and affirmed.

*Receiving and achieving.* Work is a significant issue in adulthood and provides the opportunity for gain. What adults do with their gains in life and what they think about them quickly mature into theological issues. Some people amass significant gain from their work; the resources so acquired can be viewed as the result of a gift of God or one's own efforts. Living with the sense that you were in the right place at the right time with abilities and opportunities not entirely of your own making leads to a sense of gratitude and, perhaps, a sense of stewardship. Living with the conviction that you made it on your own, pulled yourself up by your own bootstraps, built your success by yourself leads to a sense of ownership and, perhaps, entitlement. Either attitude will influence an individual's openness to grace, readiness to share, commitment to others, and sense of responsibility.

*Failure and forgiveness.* Adults have lived long enough that the dreams of things they would surely do, the commitments about things they would never do, the successes they would be, and the mistakes they would avoid have all been tested by reality in the passing of the years. For most if not all adults, their mistakes have been more evident and less subtle than they assumed they would be. Adulthood brings the opportunity for reflective persons to face their failures, and, if they are open to grace, to experience the rush of forgiveness. The higher the pile of failure, the more one can sense the need for forgiveness and observe the consequences of its sweeping presence. Children and adolescents can experience forgiveness and be renewed by its power. But it remains for adulthood, and the cumulative effects of failure, for the full impact of forgiveness to inundate life.

*Pain and redemption.* For most adults, life does bring pain: the loss of parents, the wreckage of broken dreams, marriages dissolved or never entered, children failed or never conceived, jobs lost or never obtained, a grown child's belligerence, a hope for a different world numbed by another war. The pain comes in many different forms to different adults, but for most of them it does come. Pain is not eased by forgiveness, because it grows from a different part of the human spirit and lingers after forgiveness has done its work. Pain requires redemption. It calls for the work of God that makes things new and the love of God that replaces what cannot be mended in a broken spirit. The first work of redemption is comfort, but there is more. Pain creates hungering and thirsting, and redemption brings food and drink.

*Loss and surrender.* Adulthood brings its losses as well as its gains. Physical strength and health gradually become more precarious and result in loss for many adults. A cherished possession is stolen, a favorite view of the mountain is obscured by a condominium, a meadow of childhood adventure and solace is carved up and paved over at the edge of the interstate. Few adults make it through their years without facing loss. Loss teaches adults that they do not have all the power they wish they had. Loss sometimes requires people to assume a posture of surrender. Some things cannot be changed; other things cannot be kept the same. Trying to change the unchangeable and save the unpreservable is a futile battle that pushes fatigue into despair. Surrender can be more a gift of grace than a sign of weakness.

*Adult faith.* In these last few pages, I have done what I think the adult experience of faith does. It takes the events of life, which provide the grist for adult development, and combines them with the reflective meaning-making aspects of faith to form a reinterpretation of both life and faith. The experience of life influences the faith that adults fashion, and that faith redefines the experiences of life. The redefinition happens as people learn and grow in the community of faith. Development does not stop at the edge of adulthood. It uses the lessons that life teaches to chart new courses and establish new precedents. And faith is there, becoming more mature, more embracing, more the work of God's grace and human obedience than it was in days less influenced by the accumulation of years.

## Ministry with Adults

Adults, more than any other age group in a congregation, are susceptible to very lopsided expressions of ministry. Many adults in American parishes and congregations seldom do more than attend worship or mass. In part, the busyness of life pulls them into other tasks; in part, congregations do not always plan and program for the range of adult involvements that will nurture a maturing adult faith. The areas Westerhoff has listed as part of practical theology,[14] and which have been used in the discussions of children and youth, are helpful in considering expressions of ministry with adults as well.

### *Worship Life*

Adult faith requires worship, and it is this area of practical theology in which adults are most likely to be engaged. Worship provides participation with a community of believers. It invites persons into the presence of God, carries them forward with God's future, and connects them to the community of believers who have gathered since the beginning of time.

In adulthood, the skills to worship are now comfortably in place, and the movement of life has given liturgy and symbol a reality they did not have earlier. The lessons and gospels have been read more than once, and ears can finally begin to *hear* them. Worship collects the thoughts and emotions, as well as the sensitivities and sensibilities of adult life, and places them as an offering before God. Worship becomes the recurring scene of transformation.

### *Spiritual Life*

I have talked a good bit about reflection and adult life, even though I know that many adults refuse to reflect. The kind of reflection that a life of faith needs does not require intellectual rigor as much as it requires effort. Some people live unreflectively, and the result is that faith stays more childish than it otherwise needs to be. Spiritual life is the church's disciplined reminder of the need for reflection in Christian life.

Adults can learn to reflect on life in ways that are natural and meaningful for them. The God who has spent the energy of creation making humans unique does not use the effort of redemption to remake them in one mold. Christian spirituality has many expressions and many disciplines. The task for adults includes both learning how to live as reflective persons and learning the kinds of disciplines that help them effectively to form and focus their own spirituality.

## Moral Life

Have you ever noticed how controversial moral issues are in church? People who are not familiar with church life assume it is morally monolithic. It is not. In my congregation, some of the most feather-ruffling discussions have related to moral issues. Sometimes the discussions revolve around what the proper moral position should be; at other times they deal with the actions a moral position should motivate.

Moral stands come with a price for adults. They require a change in attitudes and perception, they indict past practices at times, they create disfavor in an unredeemed world, and they sometimes worsen an adult's financial condition. All these consequences are costly for adults, and the more the cost, the greater the argument and the stronger the resistance.

American Christianity struggles with the issues of oppression and justice, war and peace, abortion prohibition and choice, capital punishment and life imprisonment, lottery income and taxation, materialism and world hunger, and nationalism and world citizenry, as well as with issues of sexual morality, personal integrity, and others. The struggle over moral issues is frequently more intense than most other struggles in church.

Adults learn from the struggle. These struggles help people to think in moral categories, to realize the actions moral conclusions invoke, and to weigh the consequences of moral commitment. Faith is nurtured as the moral dimensions of theology continue to be addressed, as people affirm or distance themselves from a position, and as they act their way into its implications.

## Pastoral Life

Adults find meaning in their faith when they express it to others. Young people aren't the only ones in the congregation who need to be mobilized for mission action or pastoral care. Adults need these opportunities to make use of what they know and what they can do in their expression of faith. Frequently, churches provide adults with an abundance of opportunities to maintain the institutional machinery of a congregation, such as committee work, but are not as inclined to structure opportunities that enable adults to express their faith in other tasks of ministry. Adults need both kinds of service.

Acts of ministry become outward and visible symbols of inward and invisible affections and commitments. As sacraments convey the unseen activity of the God who is beyond, deeds of pastoral ministry convey the commitments of faith that is within.

## Educational Life

Adults need the opportunity for Christian education experiences. They do not need to learn the story, perhaps, but life has brought them to that point where the story of the Bible and the events of their lives intersect—even collide. The point of praxis, in Thomas Groome's term,[15] exists more convincingly in adulthood than in any other era of life. Adults need settings in which they and their companions in faith can look at the biblical story in the context of their own lives and experiences.

This process requires discipline, so all the story has a chance to meet all the experiences of life. The process requires structure, so more energy can be devoted to the study than to the convening of the meeting. The process requires community, because the story of faith is never as well understood in the context of one life as it is in the context of many lives.

Adults do not outgrow their need for disciplined educational opportunities. Education provides the environment where reflection can be encouraged and where the skills it may require can be developed. Ministry that nurtures adults will provide these opportunities.

## Learning a Christian Way in the World and Growing to Maturity in Faith

It is in adulthood, when the experiences of life have intersected with the work of grace, that the learning of a lifetime matures into the knowing of faith. Adulthood does not guarantee a mature faith, but it can provide the seasoning, the curing, the fermenting that leads to an integrated and congruent way of being Christian in the world. Adults have had the opportunity to learn the lessons of faith, and some have learned them very well. The hoped-for vision of faith has become real in these adults, and they deserve careful attention.

They have learned about the feelings of faith, and their emotions are more tutored, disciplined, and accurate. As a result, they are more ready to live patiently with an openness to God. They have felt enough pain, and been surprised by enough joy, that they live with a fresh memory of God.

These adults have had the opportunity to learn the Christian story and have reflected on its themes in the trauma and triumph of the years. They learned the story as children, learned to reflect critically on it in youth, and, as adults, have lived into a vision of the world as God dreams it to be. The thoughts of faith have embraced the vision of faith, and their knowing has slipped from head to soul. They have found a way to make their world meaningful without making up a meaning.

They have been given both the responsibility and the opportunity to act in faithful ways. They have lived with their trusteeship, done their part, carried their weight, taken their turn, done their duty. They have acted, and faith has been minted into deeds that transcend words. They have learned about participation in the purposes of God as well as participation in the community of faith.

Learning and grace have done their job. And people who have lived with faith become steadfast. Having spent a lifetime responding to the grace that has pursued them, they have been transformed into something they could have never grown into or learned to be.

If you ever encounter an adult with this kind of faith, it will help your own faith. You will feel again the ineffable mystery of the love of God and the work of grace. If you wonder where some of these adults might be, I would encourage you to pay attention to the people at church. They are there, in the midst of all the others. This kind of faith will never draw much attention to itself, but if you should attend to it, you will discover the artwork of God.

# NOTES

PART ONE: Paying Attention to the Way
People of Faith Learn and Grow

1. A version of this phrase became a part of my vocabulary while reading Ernest Boyer's *A Way in the World: Family Life as a Spiritual Discipline* (San Francisco: Harper & Row, 1984). His phrase becomes, for me, a description of faith's influence on life.

Chapter 1: Paying Attention to the People at Church

1. Nicholas Hobbs, *The Troubled and Troubling Child* (San Francisco: Jossey-Bass Publishers, 1982).

2. Myron Madden, *The Power to Bless* (Nashville: Broadman Press, 1968).

3. Carol Gilligan, *In a Different Voice: Psychological Theory and Women's Development* (Cambridge, Mass.: Harvard University Press, 1982), reviews some of these studies in chapter 1; Juanita Williams, *Psychology of Women: Behavior in a Biosocial Context,* 2nd ed. (New York: W. W. Norton & Co., 1983), provides a similar review in chapter 6.

4. An example of a major survey study in which region of country was relatively nonpredictive of any of the attitudes or beliefs expressed by participants can be found in D. Schuller, M. Strommen, and M. Brekke, eds., *Ministry in America* (San Francisco: Harper & Row, 1980), especially chapter 4.

5. Erik Erikson's most recent restatement of his seminal theory of development can be found in *The Life Cycle Completed: A Review* (New York: W. W. Norton & Co., 1982).

## Chapter 2: Paying Attention to the Way of Faith

1. My image reflects a position, although informally taken, on the structure-content issues in faith development theory. For me, the phenomenon called "faith" is not limited to Christianity. But content influences structures, it does not just reside within them. So the character of faith may vary from one believing tradition to another. I will deal with the contents and structure of Christian faith.

2. Craig Dykstra and J. Harry Fernhout, in two essays in *Faith Development and Fowler,* raise questions about "What is faith?" and "Where is faith?" I'm using the questions in this chapter to raise the issues; they have raised the questions to argue particular positions. Their essays have helped me to think in these terms. See Craig Dykstra and Sharon Parks, eds., *Faith Development and Fowler* (Birmingham, Ala.: Religious Education Press, 1986).

3. The distinction between faith "out there" and faith "in here" attempts to reflect a part of the distinction that George Lindbeck makes between doctrine which functions as "informative propositions or truth claims about objective realities" and doctrine which functions as "noninformative and nondiscursive symbols of inner feelings, attitudes, or existential orientations." See George A. Lindbeck, *The Nature of Doctrine: Religion and Theology in a Postliberal Age* (Philadelphia: Westminster Press, 1984), p. 16.

4. This conception of faith is influentially argued by James Fowler, *Stages of Faith: The Psychology of Human Development and the Quest for Meaning* (San Francisco: Harper & Row, 1981).

5. This approach is shown in the work of James Fowler and in Sharon Parks, *The Critical Years: The Young Adult Search for a Faith to Live By* (San Francisco: Harper & Row, 1986).

6. Relationship is a central issue in Fowler, but relationship and meaning reflect different aspects in his concept of faith and faith development.

7. Fowler would be among those who argue that faith is a human universal.

8. This position is assumed by many in revivalist traditions.

9. This is a common assumption of many of the people in the churches, although I have seldom seen it advocated in scholarly treatments.

10. I am interpreting this perspective as similar to the one Dwayne Huebner has argued in "Christian Growth in Faith" (*Religious Education,* vol. 81, no. 4 [Fall 1986], pp. 511–522).

11. This is a dominant perspective in structural-developmental theories like Fowler's.

12. C. H. Dodd, *The Epistle of Paul to the Romans* (New York: Harper & Brothers, 1932), commentary on Romans 1:16–17, p. 15.

13. Huebner, loc. cit. note 10, p. 515.

14. C. Ellis Nelson, *Where Faith Begins* (Atlanta: John Knox Press, 1967), p. 32.

15. Sara Little, *To Set One's Heart: Belief and Teaching in the Church* (Atlanta: John Knox Press, 1983), p. 17.

16. Craig Dykstra, in Dykstra and Parks, *Faith Development and Fowler,* p. 55.

17. James Fowler, "Faith and the Structuring of Meaning," in Dykstra and Parks, *Faith Development and Fowler,* pp. 25–26.

18. Parks, *The Critical Years,* p. 16.

19. Fowler, *Stages of Faith,* pp. 92–93.

20. James Loder, *The Transforming Moment: Understanding Convictional Experiences* (San Francisco: Harper & Row, 1981), uses this term (see chapter 1).

21. James Fowler in *Stages of Faith* and Sharon Parks in *The Critical Years* both use this term.

## Chapter 3: Learning in the Community of Faith

1. Parker Palmer, *To Know as We Are Known: A Spirituality of Education* (San Francisco: Harper & Row, 1983), p. 8.

2. The characterizations in this paragraph are drawn, respectively, from Thomas Groome, *Christian Religious Education: Sharing Our Story and Vision* (San Francisco: Harper & Row, 1980); Craig Dykstra, *Vision and Character: A Christian Educator's Alternative to Kohlberg* (Ramsey, N.J.: Paulist Press, 1981); Parker Palmer, *To Know as We Are Known;* and Donald Miller, *Story and Context: An Introduction to Christian Education* (Nashville: Abingdon Press, 1987).

3. James Dittes, unpublished paper prepared for Search Institute, Minneapolis, as part of a study funded by the National Endowment for the Humanities, March 1978.

4. Carl R. Rogers, *Freedom to Learn for the 80's* (Columbus, Ohio: Charles E. Merrill Publishing Co., 1983), p. 124.

5. See, for example, the work cited in "Researching Person-centered Issues in Education," in Rogers, *Freedom to Learn for the 80's,* pp. 197–224; and data reported by Robert Horowitz, "Effects of the Open Classroom," in Herbert Walberg, ed., *Educational Environments and Effects* (Berkeley, Calif.: McCutchan Publishing Corp., 1979).

6. Robert Webber, *Secular Humanism: Threat and Challenge* (Grand Rapids: Zondervan Publishing House, 1982), is one example.

7. B. F. Skinner presents the most complete account of behaviorist theory in *Science and Human Behavior* (New York: Macmillan Co., 1953).

8. See, for example, Albert Bandura, *Social Learning Theory* (Englewood Cliffs, N.J.: Prentice-Hall, 1977).

9. Ibid.

10. Daryl Bem, *Beliefs, Attitudes, and Human Affairs* (Belmont, Calif.: Brooks/Cole Publishing Co., 1970).

11. These ideas are drawn primarily from Jerome Bruner, *Toward a Theory of Instruction* (New York: W. W. Norton & Co., 1966). See also Jerome Bruner, *The Process of Education* (New York: Random House, 1960).

12. Bruner, *Process of Education,* pp. 8–15.

13. The movement toward narrative approaches to theology, biblical studies, and practical theology is perhaps the most widespread movement in Christian scholarly traditions of the last part of the twentieth century. A number of Christian educators, including Groome, Dykstra, and Miller as well as a host of others, provide detailed analysis of the story's place in Christian education.

14. Sara Little, in *To Set One's Heart: Belief and Teaching in the Church* (Atlanta: John Knox Press, 1983), provides significant discussion about critical thought and reflection.

15. James Fowler, in *Stages of Faith: The Psychology of Human Development and the Quest for Meaning* (San Francisco: Harper & Row, 1981), argues for the importance of imagination in faith, as does Sharon Parks in "Imagination and Spirit in Faith Development," in Dykstra and Parks, eds., *Faith Development and Fowler* (Birmingham, Ala.: Religious Education Press, 1986).

16. Thomas Kuhn, *The Structure of Scientific Revolutions* (Chicago: University of Chicago Press, 1970).

17. David Kolb, *Experiential Learning: Experience as the Source of Learning and Development* (Englewood Cliffs, N.J.: Prentice-Hall, 1984).


## Chapter 4: Growing in the Community of Faith

1. This model reflects some concepts for a social learning theory of development. See, for example, Albert Bandura, *Social Learning Theory* (Englewood Cliffs, N.J.: Prentice-Hall, 1977). While the dependency anxiety is appropriate for a child of this age, the concept of separation anxiety can last into adulthood. See John Bowlby, *Attachment and Loss* (New York: Basic Books, 1969).

2. This model reflects a kind of behavioral learning concept of development, although it is meant in a much less rigid way than formal behavioral theory.

3. This approach toward development is meant to represent the position Robert Kegan takes in *The Evolving Self: Problem and Process in Human Development* (Cambridge, Mass.: Harvard University Press, 1982).

4. This description is meant to reflect the position Urie Bronfenbrenner presents in *The Ecology of Human Development* (Cambridge, Mass.: Harvard University Press, 1979).

5. Erik Erikson, *Childhood and Society* (New York: W. W. Norton & Co., 1950, 1963).

6. John B. Watson, "The Behaviorist Looks at Instincts," *Harper's Magazine,* July 1927.

7. See, for example, Sidney Bijou and Donald Baer, *Child Development,* vol. 1: *A Systematic and Empirical Theory* (New York: Appleton-Century-Crofts, 1961).

8. Bronfenbrenner, *The Ecology of Human Development.*

9. See Jean Piaget and Bärbel Inhelder, *The Psychology of the Child,* tr. by H. Weaver (New York: Basic Books, 1969).

10. A social learning approach to development is presented by Albert Bandura in *Social Learning Theory.*

11. James Fowler, *Stages of Faith: The Psychology of Human Development and the Quest for Meaning* (San Francisco: Harper & Row, 1981).

12. G. Temp Sparkman, *The Salvation and Nurture of the Child of God: The Story of Emma* (Valley Forge, Pa.: Judson Press, 1983).

13. Huebner argues this position in an essay entitled "Christian Growth in Faith" (*Religious Education,* vol. 81, no. 4 [Fall 1986], pp. 511–522).

## Chapter 5: Children of Faith and the Community of Faith

1. Martin Buber, *Between Man and Man,* tr. by R. G. Smith (New York: Macmillan Publishing Co., 1965), p. 83.

2. These interviews were not the precisely worded, technically scored kind of work that James Fowler has reported in *Stages of Faith* (San Francisco: Harper & Row, 1981), or that David Heller has reported in *The Children's God* (Chicago: University of Chicago Press, 1986). They are conversations used to illustrate a perspective on faith and do not reflect any approach toward measurement, although some of the questions were taken from these interviews.

3. James Fowler, in *Stages of Faith,* and Ronald Goldman, in *Religious Thinking from Childhood to Adolescence* (New York: Seabury Press, 1964), have both documented some of the differences.

4. I do not propose this perspective as a competing alternative to the careful work of theorists such as James Fowler. These conversations, and the experience of faith conveyed by these two boys, can be accurately evaluated in Fowler's stages of intuitive-projective and mythic-literal faith.

## Chapter 6: Paying Attention to Children

1. Iris Cully, in *Christian Child Development* (San Francisco: Harper & Row, 1979), is among those persons who makes this point. See especially chapter 3.

2. This is an interpretation of the influences of cognitive development on emotionality and is based on the theory of Robert Kegan, *The Evolving Self: Problem and Process in Human Development* (Cambridge, Mass.: Harvard University Press, 1982), chapter 5.

3. This description also reflects Robert Kegan's analysis and is discussed in *The Evolving Self,* chapter 6.

4. This description is drawn from the theory of Erik Erikson, *Childhood and Society* (New York: W. W. Norton & Co., 1950, 1963), pp. 258–261.

5. This analysis summarizes aspects of an influential theory of cognitive development proposed by Jean Piaget. See, for example, Jean Piaget and Bärbel Inhelder, *The Psychology of the Child,* tr. by H. Weaver (New York: Basic Books, 1969).

6. These characteristics are part of a stage of cognitive development frequently described as concrete operational thought.

7. James Fowler, *Stages of Faith: The Psychology of Human Development and the Quest for Meaning* (San Francisco: Harper & Row, 1981), p. 133.

8. G. Temp Sparkman, *The Salvation and Nurture of the Child of God: The Story of Emma* (Valley Forge, Pa.: Judson Press, 1983); see especially chapter 2.

9. Ibid., chapter 3.

10. See William Hendricks, *A Theology for Children* (Nashville: Broadman Press, 1980).

11. Ibid., p. 11.

12. John Westerhoff, *Building God's People in a Materialistic Society* (New York: Seabury Press, 1983), p. 9.

13. Iris Cully, *Christian Child Development,* pp. 151–152.

## Chapter 7: Paying Attention to Youth

1. David Bakan, in "Adolescence in America: From Idea to Social Fact" (*Daedalus,* Fall 1971), has convincingly argued how adolescence has emerged in American society as a social and cultural invention.

2. Definitions of adolescence are offered in most texts on adolescent development; see, for example, John Conger, *Adolescence and Youth: Psychological Development in a Changing World* (San Francisco: Harper & Row, 1977). I have characterized adolescence elsewhere as beginning "with the emergence of physiological characteristics that result in puberty. It is accompanied by the social attitudes and expectations that an individual is something other than a child. Adolescence draws to a close as persons begin to assume adult tasks such as work, self-support, marriage, or emotional independence from parents" (*Understanding Today's Youth* [Nashville: Convention Press, 1982], pp. 28–29).

3. See, for example, Erik Erikson, *Identity, Youth, and Crisis* (New York: W. W. Norton & Co., 1968).

4. Helmut Thielicke, in *Being Human . . . Becoming Human* (Garden City, N.Y.: Doubleday & Co., 1984), pp. 37–62, draws this analysis from the three kinds of despair about which Søren Kirkegaard philosophized.

5. See Jean Piaget and Bärbel Inhelder, *The Psychology of the Child,* tr. by H. Weaver (New York: Basic Books, 1969), pp. 141–144, for a basic description of formal operational thought.

6. Mihaly Csikszentmihalyi and Reed Larson, *Being Adolescent: Conflict and Growth in the Teenage Years* (New York: Basic Books, 1984).

7. Ibid., p. 59.

8. Peter L. Benson, Dorothy Williams, and Arthur Johnson, *The Quicksilver Years: The Hopes and Fears of Early Adolescence* (San Francisco: Harper & Row, 1987), p. 183.

9. Ibid., pp. 29–30.

10. Csikszentmihalyi and Larson, *Being Adolescent,* pp. 155–160.

11. These figures are from additional analysis of *Monitoring the Future* data for 1984–85, conducted by Dean Hoge for the Youth Ministry and Theological Schools project funded by the Lilly Endowment and directed by Sara Little, January 1987.

12. G. Temp Sparkman, *The Salvation and Nurture of the Child of God: The Story of Emma* (Valley Forge, Pa.: Judson Press, 1983), pp. 109, 111.

13. James Fowler, in *Stages of Faith: The Psychology of Human Development and the Quest for Meaning* (San Francisco: Harper & Row, 1981), describes this as synthetic-conventional faith.

14. This information was abstracted from the Search Institute periodic publication *Source,* January 1986.

15. See, for example, Merton and Irene Strommen, *Five Cries of Parents* (San Francisco: Harper & Row, 1985), especially chapter 5.

16. This conclusion comes from an analysis of Search Institute data from 1971 to 1979.

17. Thanks to Mark Johnson for making his statement available for inclusion in this chapter.

### Chapter 8: Paying Attention to Adults

1. Erik Erikson's theory overview has been most recently stated in his *The Life Cycle Completed: A Review* (New York: W. W. Norton & Co., 1982).

2. D. Levinson, C. Darrow, E. Klein, M. Levinson, and B. McKee, *The Seasons of a Man's Life* (New York: Alfred A. Knopf, 1978), and G. E. Vaillant, *Adaptation to Life* (New York: Little, Brown & Co., 1977).

3. Development as a process of learning is reflected in work such as Albert Bandura, *Social Learning Theory* (Englewood Cliffs, N.J.: Prentice-Hall, 1977). See also Urie Bronfenbrenner, *The Ecology of Human Development* (Cambridge, Mass.: Harvard University Press, 1979).

4. James Dittes, *When Work Goes Sour* (Philadelphia: Westminster Press, 1987).

5. See, for example, Jesus' teaching in the Sermon on the Mount (Matt. 6:24).

6. For example, see Carol Gilligan, *In a Different Voice: Psychological Theory and Women's Development* (Cambridge, Mass.: Harvard University Press, 1982).

7. Some of these arguments are summarized in Juanita Williams, *Psychology of Women: Behavior in a Biosocial Context,* 2nd ed. (New York: W. W. Norton & Co., 1983), especially chapters 5 and 6.

8. See particularly James Dittes, *The Male Predicament: On Being a Man Today* (San Francisco: Harper & Row, 1985).

9. Carol Gilligan, *In a Different Voice.*

10. James Fowler, in *Becoming Adult, Becoming Christian* (San Francisco: Harper & Row, 1984), provides the most thorough discussion of the implications of faith-stages theory for adults.

11. G. Temp Sparkman, *The Salvation and Nurture of the Child of God: The Story of Emma* (Valley Forge, Pa.: Judson Press, 1983), chapter 5.

12. Gabriel Moran, *Religious Education Development* (Minneapolis: Winston Press, 1983), pp. 171–173.

13. Ibid., pp. 204–205.

14. John Westerhoff, *Building God's People in a Materialistic Society* (New York: Seabury Press, 1983).

15. Thomas Groome, *Christian Religious Education* (San Francisco: Harper & Row, 1980), particularly chapter 9.